ENDORSEMENTS

It's time for a new breed of seller who inspires clients to change. Get this book to discover how to become an invaluable, irresistible resource and at the same time close more profitable sales.

Jill Konrath, Bestselling author of SNAP Selling and Agile Selling

"We all accept, at least I hope we do, that the art of conversation appears to be dying, as we prefer to develop our relationships online. This is certainly true when it comes to our commercial interactions as more and more products and solutions become commoditized. But the very best performers in the sales space, the ones who consistently over-achieve, have developed their communication skills and they are leaving their competitors trailing in the distance. Bernadette McClelland provides us with a superbly written guide, which should be a must-read for anyone with aspirations to become a top 5% player in the game of sales."

Jonathan Farrington, Founder & CEO of Top Sales World

"Bernadette McClelland's new book *The Art of Commercial Conversations* hit me hard like a Bondi wave - refreshing, invigorating and powerful. She has encapsulated the changing world of doing business with business - a world where the buyer has transformed the way they are doing business which necessitates that sellers rethink how they engage. She states that we can no longer succeed by being sellers, we need to be Changemakers - we need to sell change. I totally agree. This book is essential reading for every business leader and sales professional in the business to business world".

John Smibert, Co-Founder of Sales Masterminds Australasia

"Bernadette's new book offers fresh insights into organising, structuring and leading client conversations in today's crazy busy world. It has the goal of accelerating understanding, while creating a foundation of respect and trust in a climate of mutual learning. Every chapter is dense-packed with actionable information that any reader, no matter how advanced, will be able to benefit from."

Gerhard Gschwandtner, Founder and CEO,
Selling Power Inc.

"*The Art of Commercial Conversations* is one of the most inspirational yet strategic books I have read in the sales space. The ability for a salesperson to ask questions of the buyer but also themselves is critical, to be able to have a commercial dialogue and not a sales monologue is crucial and the knowledge that there is an art and a science to selling and dancing with both is key. I highly recommend every professional with a responsibility for generating revenue read this book today".

Alice Heiman, Business Management Consultant,
Emcee and Chief Networking Officer for Sales 2.0 Conference

"Bernadette McClelland, in *The Art of Commercial Conversations*, creates a solid manifesto to lead the way into Sales 3.0. She skilfully guides the reader to understand, process and embrace mastering the philosophy and skills of conscious selling, the new selling paradigm. Bernadette brings the reader clarity of thought and a solid selling process, desperately needed in today's globally competitive business ecosystem. Clearly, the sellers who triumph are those who understand not only who their buyer is but have also taken the time to understand who they are, themselves. That breadth and depth of honest understanding is the fulcrum of the art of value creation. I strongly recommend this book to sellers of all levels."

Babette Ten Haken, Management Strategist &
Business Coach, Author, Do YOU Mean Business?
A Playbook for Cross-Functional Collaboration

"Bernadette McClelland has written a timely and timeless masterpiece. Enlightened leadership is needed more than ever, especially in an industry that is losing its way. This is a must read for everyone in professional selling who aspires to a values driven approach to leadership and seeking a framework for making a difference through integrity, passion and value."

Tony J. Hughes, Keynote Speaker, Best Selling Author,
B2B Social Selling Commentator

Reading Bernadette's book is like being around her - inspirational, thoughtful, and focused on growth. In *"The Art of Commercial Conversations"* she invites sellers to rethink their approach with buyers and to value conviction, context, and contribution. This ties in strongly with how the role of sales has changed, and the book speaks to that. Buy the book and hone the craft of professional conversations - it is a lifeline in a sea of business change.

Lori Richardson, CEO, Score More Sales
& President, Women Sales Pros

Social technologies have turbo-charged the expectations of today's hyper-connected consumer. All parts of the marketing process are being impacted, and none more so than sales. But technology is just the enabler. Today, marketing and all it entails is about being human, taking a heart-centred approach, telling stories, creating conversations and becoming part of our customers' communities. In *The Art of Commercial Conversations*, Bernadette McClelland challenges us to change the way we think about sales and selling, what can we do to ensure we're more in-sync with today's buyers? Ask yourself: "What are the conversations you are having?"

Trevor Young, Author: microDOMINATION
and Founder of Digital Citizen and PR Warrior

Because technology has changed the nature of communities, it has changed the nature of business and as a result brands and individuals must adapt and engage with even more connective purpose. People have always bought from people they know, like, and trust and these nine conversations within *The Art of Commercial Conversations* definitely expound the importance of that engagement message.

Jill Rowley, International Speaker,
Social Selling Evangelist, Forbes Top 30 Sales People

Having a noble purpose aligns so much to a salespersons intention to serve and ultimately sell. *The Art of Commercial Conversations* frames nine 'must have' conversations that sales people and business owners need to have with their potential clients, and themselves, in order for business prosperity and profitability to occur. This book is a refreshing take on how the world of business is shifting to be one that focuses on contribution as well as growth.

Lisa Earle McLeod, Bestselling Author of 'Selling with Noble Purpose'
and Sales Leadership Expert for Forbes.com

I have had the great pleasure of watching Bernadette present her unique brand of sales thinking to a live sales audience several times now. The one thing that stands out about her Conscious Selling Model is how easily it can be woven into the fabric of a sales process to create a new level of thinking which is truly transformational. As it transforms thinking, it immediately transforms the actions of the sales team to produce improved results as they engage their customer. *The Art of Commercial Conversations* will be a must have resource for any size sales team that wants to take their game to the next level.

Mark Dinunzio~ President, MarketPoint Solutions

"In *The Art of Commercial Conversations* – When It's Your Turn To Make A Difference, Bernadette McClelland has written the new Bible of selling. Packed with practical advice, knowledge, personal experience and wisdom this is the only Sales Book you need on your shelf. If you believe in the power of business to transform and its purpose to serve, then this book will help you make the difference you were born to make."

Brooke Alexander, Founder and Author
of Your Legacy Project

THE ART OF COMMERCIAL CONVERSATIONS

Drive Revenue. Increase Margin.
Sell A Difference.

BERNADETTE MCCLELLAND

The Art of Commercial Conversations

Published by Be Bold Publishing
PO Box 318, Sunbury
Victoria 3429 Australia

The National Library of Australia
McClelland, Bernadette
The Art of Commercial Conversations:
Drive Revenue. Increase Margin. Sell A Difference.
ISBN   paperback   978-0-9873561-2-3
          ebook   978-0-9873561-3-0

Cover Design By: Tim McClelland

Typesetting and Editing By: Jake Muelle

Author's Note
Throughout this book, the word 'he' has been used at times when referring to customer or salesperson. The use of this word does not imply any gender superiority or inferiority. The word customer has been used when referring to client as well.

Printed and bound in Australia by:
Inscope Books,
287 Military Road, Cremorne,
Sydney, NSW 2090

"Art isn't only a painting. Art is anything that's creative, passionate, and personal. And great art resonates with the viewer, not only with the creator.

An artist is someone who uses bravery, insight, creativity, and boldness to challenge the status quo. And an artist takes it personally.

Art is a personal gift that changes the recipient. The medium doesn't matter. The intent does.

Art is a personal act of courage, something one human does that creates change in another.'

Seth Godin

CONTENTS

BOOK ONE

POSITION! - The Value of You and
Your Personal Leadership

BOOK TWO
THINK! - The Value of Your Offering
and Your Thought Leadership

BOOK THREE
SELL! - The Value To Your Market and
Your Sales Leadership

ACKNOWLEDGEMENTS

T HIS PART OF the book is the easiest and yet the most difficult. Easy, because I am so grateful to the people who have helped me in developing my thoughts and collating them into some semblance of order, and difficult because these few words of gratitude and appreciation don't seem enough for their level of contribution and influence.

By writing this book my purpose is to contribute in my unique way to shift the perception of the sales role and elevate the profession of selling. To help sellers, leaders and business owners realise there is nothing difficult about having commercial conversations or initiating conversations that sell, when you have the right intention.

There is simply the diversity of people you are working with, their beliefs, their aspirations, their perceptions and expectations as well as those of your own. It means to be more successful and effective, you may need to expand *your* learnings and shift *your* thinking as well.

When we realise that our commercial conversations are really not about us at all, then the whole purpose of our discussions become easier and more meaningful. When we realise we really are there to serve and be a conduit for the growth of our buyer's business and ultimately, their lives, it gives these conversations purpose.

Special thanks to the women I surround myself with and travel halfway around the world to hang out with every year, Women Sales Pros led by the ever-inspiring Lori Richardson.

For the words of gut-wrenching honesty by Jill Konrath (SNAP Selling and Agile Selling) who unwittingly challenged me over a dinner in Seattle to step up and play the biggest game she knew I was capable of playing.

To the thousands of people on the BernadetteMcClelland.com blog, LinkedIn and other sites who read my words regularly and provide feedback, uptake and the support of my ideas, thank you.

To my male colleagues in the world of professional sales, thank you. Especially advocates such as Larry Levine (Selling from the Heart) and Anthony Iannarino, Jeb Blount, Mark Hunter and Mike Weinberg who backed me as a speaker at Outbound, John Smibert (Strategic Selling) and Jonathan Farrington (Top Sales World).

To the girls and guys outside of the sales world who cheer me on and continue to hold me to account: the talented and service-driven Jimi Potcharnart, Founder of The Thailand Coaching Academy; my ever trusted confidante, Gail Mastrowicz and my sagacious and wonderful confidante and friend, Brooke Alexander, Founder of Your Legacy Project; Tanuja Vashistha, my partner in New Delhi, India; and my colleagues from the Tony Robbins community who are always there with an ear and heart at the ready.

To the wonderful professional women in my own exclusive mastermind group, *The Hive*, who have held me to account and to a higher standard, Tamera Lloyd Jones, Michelle Gibson, Carol Yeomans and Julie Wiggins.

World leaders such as Seth Godin, Daniel Pink and Neil Rackham whose words have made me think so differently.

There are also mentors from whom I have learned in classroom and workshop environments: Tony Robbins who influenced my personal leadership skills and allowed me the opportunity to work as his coach for Asia Pacific at a time that I needed his influence both personally and professionally. Matt Church, founder of Thought Leaders Global who influenced my thought leadership skills, helped me own my speaking platform and message, and to follow the sign that said *Stage* and not *Exit*. To my past managers and colleagues from Xerox, who for over twenty years contributed to my sales leadership skills after agreeing to back a young and naive rookie who they didn't think had what it took.

Special thanks to those rock stars shown on the previous pages who found time to read my draft copy and so generously share their thoughts on my words.

Clearly, I stand on the shoulders of giant. It is proof that no man, or woman, is an island, that we all do need a village to support us.

But the shoulders I stand on most are those of my immediate family.

My husband Tim, who would rather die than see me not achieve my dreams. The man who listened patiently to every page being read with every amendment made and still carried on with a *'you can do this'* mantra. My beautiful daughter Danielle who inspired me through her own extremely successful and respected leadership journey, having served in the Middle East with Australia's Royal Australian Airforce making the rank of Sargent, and my son, Matthew, who poked his head around the corner every now and then and said, *'Mum, when you're finished can you do some food shopping please, we have nothing to eat.'*

Writing this book has been a labour of love. I hope you love the words on the page as much as I enjoyed writing them for you.

PREFACE

HAVE YOU EVER wondered why some people are extremely successful, and why their clients love them and advocate for them at any given time? Who manage to sail through any economic downturn easily and effortlessly, yet others experience failure, stress and a loss of business growth?

Why does business building come so easily to some people and not to others?

How can you ensure you stay successful or become even more successful and respected in your role as a business person who sells?

There are many facets to being responsible for revenue growth today. Learning to get your foot in the door and closing the sale are no longer the two key skills you need on which to focus. In this book, 'The Art of Commercial Conversations', you will find fantastic insights into those conversations you must have with yourself and with others. It will join the dots for you, help you to turn the hard sell style of yesteryear into a heart sell style for tomorrow, yet still drive revenue today. It will help you realise you are in exactly the right place at the right time.

'*The Art of Commercial Conversations*' is about changing the perception of selling. It's about changing **your** perception of selling. It is about becoming who you need to be as much as learning what you need to do, why you need to do it or even how you will go about achieving those results.

With buyers taking control of the sales conversation, with caveat emptor losing its impetus and with sellers at a loose end not knowing what to do to win the business, now is a perfect time to realise what you might be missing. There is no time like the present adjust and adopt a new level conversation to achieve those results that matter the most.

Bernadette McClelland, December 2018

FIVE FASCINATING WORDS

AS I SIT here about to start thousands of keystrokes, I am in my favourite coffee lounge. I'm looking out the window, sorting my thoughts and prioritising a mish-mash of different concepts. And then, from behind me, I hear five simple words:

"How Can I Help You?"

And at that point I think, *'That's it! That's my entire book written!'*

It doesn't matter what training course we've done, what seminars we've attended, what books we've read – how we position ourselves, how we think and how we frame what it is we sell, is key. Our thinking therefore becomes central to our results. Our thinking is what triggers our intentions, our behaviours and our actions.

As the great French philosopher René Descartes said, "I think, therefore I am."

And like my ever-accommodating barista, as sales leaders we must also position ourselves to think and have an intention to serve our potential buyers. Not just to serve the world's best skinny lattes, but to help, to assist, to collaborate, to contribute, to sell.

If anyone wants to know how to open a conversation or close a deal, simply reflect on those five words, *'How Can I Help You?'*

Game over!

If only it was so simple though, in this sometimes-complicated tapestry of everyday life. The facts remain that for those who don't learn to join the dots and adopt the new rules of doing business today, they will lose the game. Selling with an intention to truly serve and contribute, to provide relevant context in conversations and to come from a space of total conviction, clarity and certainty through real connections are the new rules of engagement.

Game Set and Match!

The Shift We Can't Ignore

I want you to ask yourself:

- Do you think the sales landscape is as simple as it once was or is it getting so much more complex?
- Do you think the expectation of buyers is staying the same or rapidly increasing?
- Do you think it's easier for sales environments today to compete or is it getting harder?

I can hazard a guess. You don't think, you *know*!

It IS getting more complex, it IS changing at a rapid rate and it IS getting even tougher out there!

In the past sellers had the certain luxury of automatically churning their products when it was financially viable, rolling over their services into the next contract, effortlessly enticing the buyer to sign on the dotted line by dangling attractive, yet scarcity-based *deal breakers* that had to be signed by close of business that day.

Today, though, we know the tables have turned. The buyers hold the cards. The buyers know more than us in many cases, thanks to the advent of technology. They're up to scratch on NLP techniques; they've been taught how to sell, and in many instances, are more educated. Sellers today need to stop reacting by trying to manage this change that is happening because it is placing them behind the eight ball. Instead they need to become more proactive, become bolder and be responsible for creating their own change.

The three key areas you, as a seller, must consider taking more ownership, includes your positioning in how you approach the market, the way you think about your commercial conversations and your selling styles so that the outcomes are a win/win/win dynamic.

The competitor is no longer the business around the corner or the guy sitting in his Porsche down the road. The new competition is the status quo. It's actually a little word called '*maybe.*' What that means is that buyers prefer to stay with what they have, complete with its perceived and known misgivings, rather than risk disrupting the status quo and making change happen, placing them into even more uncertainty.

It's About Change

Sellers today have to forget about selling their showroom or catalogue products as they know them to be. Change is their new product, service or idea. It's about having the skills and insights to **make** change happen for them and their buyer. We are no longer sellers, we are changemakers and we sell change! This is such a different concept for many to get their heads around and to do that is to position yourself exclusively, think laterally and sell consciously by tapping into your personal leadership, thought leadership and sales leadership skills. It's your Leadership Triad.

The Leadership Triad underpins the Conscious Selling Model and is reliant on both external and internal resources. The Conscious Selling Model embodies modern day philosophies and provides answers on how sellers can shift and improve their mindset and skillset in order to play a bigger game. It is based on nine commercial conversations and is about not just surviving, but also thriving, in today's shifting business landscape. Today, it's no longer about just doing a deal, it's about being the real deal and that starts with you.

Yesterday, Today and Tomorrow

Charles Darwin said it best, *'It is not the strongest or the most intelligent who will survive but those who can best manage change.'* It's more than managing change, its making change happen by aspiring to something deeper, broader and higher.

This model provides an aspirational and measurable path that allows a seller to see where they are against world's best practice, where they can map out their own professional path.

If we go back in time, not quite as far back as the bartering economy, but definitely as far back as the world Alec Baldwin introduced us to in the movie Glengarry Glen Ross, the mantra that got our attention was *'ABC: Always be Closing.'*

It was an approach that made even our beloved Jehovah Witnesses hide behind their curtains when they saw a seller coming, and this approach was also so humorously epitomised in the YouTube clip where the affable Kenny sells his cleaning products door to door.

THE CONSCIOUS SELLING MODEL

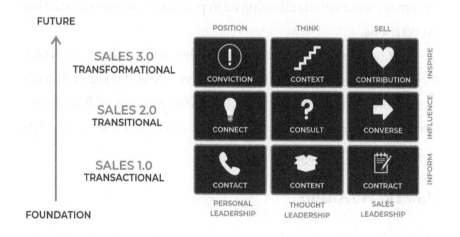

© BERNADETTE MCCLELLAND

The process we have used for eons has always had a baseline that flows from contacting our prospect. Next we were taught to deliver our content through the features, advantages and benefits of our solution, and demonstrate our expertise by being the walking, talking encyclopaedia that loved talking about the product. Then we closed for the deal. *This process categorised as Sales 1.0 was, and still is in many instances, very transactional and very informational.*

In the 1980's we moved to a more relationship based, solution sell. *Sales 2.0 was based on relationships and influencing* our clients through questionning skills was introduced. The research undertaken by Neil Rackham over twelve years, including the observation of thirty-five thousand sales calls demonstrated what separated the successful from the rest. This resulted in the SPIN selling methodology being born. It was a gamechanger that re-invented the face of sales at the time, taught us how to connect with our buyers by creating rapport and led us into the consultative questionning framework that deepened customer conversations allowing us to pivot off customer satisfaction expectations.

And now we find ourselves at another fork in the road, where these processes alone are not enough. Even Neil Rackham himself says of the current day scenario, *'The changing face of B2B buying behaviour is affecting every stage of the sales process – vendors must adapt or they will become irrelevant.'*

How Do We Adapt?

It's not about farmers or hunters these days. Sure, farmers sow the seed and nurture and cultivate the relationships but that's not enough. It's also not enough to call up for the sole reason of asking, *'how are you going?'*, or worse turn up with coffee and donuts because you want to while away some time. People don't want overpaid courier services wasting their precious time.

And what about the hunters? Those who get their energy off the hunt, make the kill and move on? Businesses are saying **no more!** We don't want to be sold to; we want someone to help us make a difference in our business. And as we find ourselves at that fork, like most changemakers, only the ones who take the road less travelled will succeed.

It's more than **doing** and **having**. *Sales 3.0 is transformational and inspirational* and more about **being**. It is definitely the road less travelled for the common seller because it's about customer intimacy and people being more human with each other. It's about reaching a place where your approach is transformational for you, your business and the buyer. It's redefining the ABC's – to *Always Be Contributing*. Having the ability to inspire your client to **want** to make change happen by having the right approach, creating the right focus within conversations and having an intention for the outcome to be a win/win/win, is not only powerful, it's what today's clients actually want.

Where do you sit on this Conscious Selling Model? Where would you rate your ability to position, think and sell?

- Would you class yourself as transactional, transitional or transformational?
- Informational, influential or inspirational?
- Someone who is all about having, doing or being more?

The Path Less Travelled

Dan Pink in his book SWITCH, paints the picture of the elephant and the rider in describing the challenges for any of us in making change happen in our own lives. The rider thinks he is in control, sitting atop the big beast, prodding it and manoeuvring its head until the elephant decides to ignore the rider's request and go down its own path. Regardless of what we try differently, the elephant is now in control.

In this scenario, the elephant is a metaphor for our emotions, and the rider, a metaphor for our logic. It demonstrates that no matter what we choose to do, no matter how we slice or dice it – emotions win out over logic every time. And the same metaphor can be used for the sales process.

Sellers have been the rider for so many years, taking the buyer down their own path with their own seller centric agenda. After years of prodding and manoeuvring, the elephant is now taking over. The elephant, representing the new buyer, is now veering off the well-worn route and taking the seller down a new and unfamiliar path. Many sellers, though, aren't ready.

The Real Competition

The new breed of seller needs to be able to get in and out of a customer's time poor world with precision and still stay relevant on the customer's radar. That person needs to be someone who will inspire and transform a business and the people within it, and also be able to lead the sale to a profitable conclusion.

When I look back over my career I can categorically say that the successful sellers have all had in common the qualities of precision questioning, calling it as it is, having an opinion and in some cases, they have been willing to rock the boat and be bold, because they cared. The ones that rocked the boat for monetary gain alone though, have long since disappeared.

Being bold in the context of *the art of commercial conversations* doesn't just mean being brave, courageous and taking risks, it also means challenging old ways of our own thinking, challenging our customer's way of thinking and challenging the status quo. And the status quo is every seller's biggest competitor today! The sooner sellers can understand they are really selling change, and not their product, service or idea, the more value driven conversations they'll enjoy.

The journey for sellers today is all about being aspirational – it's about moving from that transactional and informational level, through the transitional stages of connecting and influencing others and stepping up yet again to a higher and more generously strategic level of business acumen.

For those that are already strong in connecting and relationship building, it's about taking their value up a rung and that can only happen when someone increases their self-awareness and is prepared to challenge their own status quo. That's when **inspiring** real change occurs. It's about taking that skillset and mindset and transforming their customers' worlds. Similar to a romantic relationship (minus the obvious), business is all about giving that which you most want. We have got to give that thing first in business, if that's what we want in return from our customers. Want respect? Give respect. Want higher margins? Giver higher value. Want awesome incomes? Give awesome outcomes.

A great example of a business that is ready and willing to adapt to this change is Marque Lawyers in Sydney, Australia. Their whole selling model has changed in order to put the customer first, and they are well and truly walking their talk. How do lawyers traditionally sell? They charge for their time. What is the biggest bugbear for a lawyer's client? The more hours clocked up on phone calls, emails and messages equate to thousands of dollars spent. Founding partner, Michael Bradley has banished the entire concept of those traditional and historic timesheets and instead charges a fixed fee or retainer. This whole philosophy is based around those five key words *'How Can I Help You?'*

So How Do We Know What Our Buyers Actually Want From Us?

We can't answer that question ourselves because the only ones who can are our buyers. By taking a general view from a recent survey, the top three factors buyers are telling us are important to them are - engagement, connection and communication.

According to The Synergy Group research, the top challenge for buyers today is increased competition while their number one priority is to win new customers. How will you help your customers achieve their priorities and overcome their challenges? It doesn't matter what you are selling, as someone making a difference, how will you contribute to your buyers winning new customers and how will you know you have succeeded?

The way that we need to address the issue of businesses not achieving their corporate revenue goals is not by knocking on more doors, not by closing more deals that aren't ready to be closed, not by reducing the price unnecessarily – it's by addressing those three key categories of improvement where the **3 major shifts need to occur -** the way that you **position** you and the value you have in yourself (Personal Leadership), the way that you **think** and how you articulate the value of your offering (Thought Leadership) and the way you **sell** though the outcomes you expect and execute in bringing your value to the market (Sales Leadership).

People are beginning to see that the old way of selling with the new informed buyer, no longer works. Buyers, whilst still tasked with the buying/sales conversations, want something different, something down to earth and even though they may not be able to articulate it clearly, they will know it when they see it. They will hear it and feel it and they will notice it in the people that are tasked with helping them buy. People like you.

Are you even aware of the conversations you are having, or not having?

I HAVE A DREAM

C HANGEMAKERS ABOUND THROUGHOUT history. Everywhere we look we see results from the thinking and actions of these amazing people. People who have transformed their dreams and sold their ideas.

I think that Martin Luther King was probably the epitome of a contemporary, modern-day sales person. He had an idea that would transform the world and he transferred that idea to others – in the shape of a dream, not a strategy.

August 28th, 1963 saw him address the masses with a speech that would change the way of humanity and make a huge dent in removing racial discrimination with the African Americans. His *I have a dream*' speech sold the world on how this group of people deserved the same rights as the remainder of America, regardless of the colour of their skin. This shift was highlighted a few years earlier when a young lady named Rosa Parks stood up for her rights, ignoring the demands of a white man on a downtown bus in Montgomery, Alabama, who wanted her to leave the bus because of the colour of her skin. It was from that incident Martin Luther King began to raise the conscious awareness of apartheid and began his campaign to sell change.

What was it that possessed two hundred thousand people to attend Lincoln Memorial that day to hear him speak and sell his idea? In an age where there was no technology, word spread like wildfire. The reason people followed Dr. King so vehemently was because they needed to believe in something. Just as all of us do. The power was in his mission. He had a cause.

His message was so clear, and he connected with the people at a real, genuine and authentic level. He never wavered from his message and lived by what he stood for. Ultimately, as history shows us, he was not only dedicated to serving others, but was prepared to serve at the highest level by making the ultimate, personal sacrifice.

I am not suggesting you pay such a high price. I am curious though, as to whether you have your own version of raving fans or advocates who strongly believe in and support your ideas, products or services. If so, what level of conviction and connection do you have with them and them with you?

Do your homework. Go into your database, visit your customers and find out what the cost to them would have been if they hadn't taken any action with you and agreed to, implemented or purchased your idea, product or service. Check in with them to find out the **massive** value they have received from you since. How have you changed their worlds, moved their business forward, helped them earn more money or build stronger relationships? Never underestimate the strength you have in serving others.

The Buyers are Rebelling

If you asked me what one phrase I remember from Form 4 Commerce class, (Mrs Mosley would be proud to know there was something!) it would be *'Caveat Emptor'*, or *'let the buyer beware.'* I'm sure in many instances over the years, buyers have prayed for the day to come when that mantra was reversed. When the words *'Caveat Venditor'* or *'let the seller beware'* would carry some extra weight for them. That day is now.

Today it's time for change and the people who are letting us know this are our buyers. They have found their voice and they are voting with their silence.

Our buyers are rebelling! They're not returning our calls, not opening our emails, they are making decisions by committee, they understand the sales process better than the sales person, they're more educated generally, are hugely attention deficit and want a sense of certainty and security. They perceive value differently, will do their homework first and make excuses more than ever.

I'm a seller, like you, even though I might masquerade as an author, a consultant, a coach, speaker, mentor and a trainer and even I have seen this change occur over a very short period of time. It used to be simple. We would take our business cards, our brochures and a good pair of shoes and we would knock on doors, we would make calls, we would rely on *'old mate'* relationships and we would dial for dollars. We held the cards. Not today. The only cards we hold are our potentially outdated business cards.

- Consider that 70% of buyers check their emails before they even get out of bed each morning, impacting their most sacred personal space, so why and when would they find the time to take a cold call from someone they don't even know?

- If 9% of buyers don't think sellers are worthy enough of their time (SAMA Conference) and don't want to even speak with you to put you on their calendar, how on earth are you going to get to speak to the person who will approve the purchase of your idea, product or service?
- Consider that only 3% of the market is looking for a solution right now and 97% aren't looking at all, yet you speak to every potential buyer as though they were ready to buy today. What percentage of success will you achieve with such a scattergun approach?

What's Got to Change?

The way I see it, because we can no longer control the purchasing process, we have to look at how **we** can change in order to **influence** and potentially **inspire** the purchasing process and assist the customer to buy – from us!

We can choose to stay the same, remain technically competent in our roles, continue to not get in front of the right people, continue to not make our budgets and continue to be pipped at the post because we just *don't get it* in the eyes of our buyers. Alternately, we can up the ante and realise we have to begin to think differently. The famous words *'we've always done business this way'* really are the seven most deadly words we can utter. We have to reassess **our** approach to the buyer, **our** focus on the conversations and disrupt **our** beliefs about the most important outcomes.

Our buyers will be silently self diagnosing their own business problems in their own time, doing their research on potential suppliers through all forms of social media and reference checking. They will be creating their own shortlist of vendors and going to the market when **they** are ready and not the other way around. This will be creating so much angst and frustration amongst sales businesses because the familiarity of those traditional sales steps have been disrupted, causing many sellers to wonder how to gain that control back.

The Corporate Executive Board (CEB) tells us that the seller is needed in the buying process later in the buying cycle. If sellers today aren't aware of how to get front of mind or capture mindshare early in the piece, then they have lost their competitive advantage. If they aren't able to incorporate *the art of commercial conversations*, or be agile enough to change their conversations, if the only reference they have is to ask questions based on an older sales methodology, their lack of relevance will make them vulnerable to an unexpected exit. But that doesn't mean it's time to pack up and go home.

This situation actually provides the smart sellers with the opportunity to reassess and start communicating in a different and more effective way. It provides the opportunity for sellers to be more innovative and identify where their conversations need to shift, what they need to add and possibly what they need to let go, when it comes to the way they do business.

Innovation and Agility

My friend and colleague, Jill Konrath, highlights in her book *'Agile Selling'* how sellers need to be more flexible. She writes, *"In a world of continuous change and perceived product/service parity, sellers are the key differentiator. Their learning agility becomes a key factor in their success."*

If a salamander can innovate by losing a limb and then replace it with a new limb within a couple of weeks, then what's preventing a seller from doing something similar - losing one behaviour and replacing it with a new set of behaviours in as short a timeframe? They can! Today it's referred to as agility, a key business resource.

Sometimes, what might be a different way of viewing this reality would be to consider what might be better for us to actually lose. Perhaps something we say, think or do that we've always done, may no longer serve us. Sometimes what we think might be strength can, in actual fact, be a weakness. I have always had an enthusiastic and outgoing personality, and in business that can potentially hold me back. That gregariousness can, in some personalities, come across as inauthentic when I am actually being who I am at my core. What I need to do, especially with a CXO, is dial back the happiness gene. We all need to be flexible and make those necessary, on-the-fly behavioural changes. The ability to adjust our positioning approach, our thought processes and selling style is crucial.

Many of us focus so much on what we need to **add** to our repertoire or portfolio. We stress out that we don't have enough, know enough or are enough, and we constantly think we lack both external resources when it's a lack of internal resourcefulness.

In essence, it's about being agile, taking on feedback and reading the play, which is why understanding what makes people tick is so important.

The Market is Shifting

Sales today is less about making contact, spilling the content of our brochure onto the buyer's desk, and then getting the contract signed. It's more about embracing a level of conviction that screams respect and responsibility, whilst having business conversations that spread a bigger, more relevant message to help you stand out and contribute more than ever to your client's business growth, as well as yours.

It's not just value driven commercial conversations, but *'values'* driven conversations that are going to cause our buyers to be more curious about what we do, and by default you will become more valued.

What then must change?

THE BIGGER CONVERSATION

THERE IS A bigger conversation at play here. It is not about how to sell or how much to make through selling. It is for sellers to sell a difference!

We've heard the cliché – moving from a push mentality to a pull mentality. Well, I think it's more than that. I think it is changing the concept of selling from a sell and *get* approach, to a serve and *give* approach. Regardless of whether you work at a multinational corporate or are an independent micro business, we all impact each other. We are all in the business of making a difference and impacting people's lives – whether we know it or not.

On average forty-four businesses per day close their doors in the state of Victoria, Australia alone; according to the Australian Bureau of Statistics (your own community will have its own desperate numbers). By the time you have lunch each day, half of those people will have signed the relevant paperwork to close the doors to their business, and by the time you go to bed each evening all of them will have contemplated their future in one way or another. Liquidation. Bankruptcy. Suicide.

Yes. Suicide! A big statement I know!

Businesses need revenue and they rely on a consistent flow of revenue generation strategies to achieve that goal. In other words, sales as a function, saves businesses! Sales, therefore, helps save lives as well. Why do I think that?

Four years ago, we lost our business; we liquidated and went bankrupt. Bedridden for twelve months with massive liver function failure, the driver of the business (me) was no longer at the wheel. Staff slackened off, sales people went AWOL, stock was being released without correct invoices and in some cases with no invoices at all. Sales declined, and cash flow stopped. My husband was travelling regionally to try to salvage the sales, run an office, look after a sick wife, parent a fourteen-year-old boy who had stepped up to become his mum's carer, calm a daughter who was on the other side of the world serving in the Middle East in the war against terror and could do nothing to help. Before we knew it, we found ourselves deep within Australia's welfare system and one day in the back roads of country Victoria my husband drove into a forest and contemplated the unthinkable.

As sellers, we have more than a responsibility to simply push products, because it's never about our products. We all have a responsibility to make money for our companies, to make money for our clients' companies, to make money for ourselves and do so in the most ethical way possible. At the same time, it's owning the value our idea, product or service offers the world, because selling that value will make a difference to someone, somewhere. Mark my words! It's about believing in that value enough to know your customers will see fit to pay market value for your products in return, but only if you make that first sale to yourself.

Simple! *'How Can I Help You?'*

I believe a shift needs to happen in the sales world where we aspire to creating purposeful revenue growth and can lift our buyer's business, and them, as we climb. It's not about being the leader, but being a leader.

I believe many are still focusing too much on how to get their foot in the door, how to SPIN clients, how to get the quickest and cheapest deal, how to manoeuvre and manipulate and everything related to tactics and strategies and war rooms. Sure, these components are important, but there are also more important factors in selling today. We need to stop trying to *get,* and focus on those five words, *'How Can I Help You?'* The conversation has to be bigger, the message more meaningful and the outcomes more win/win/win.

Love Languages of Business

Sales as a profession should be an extension of who we are as people. We should give that which we most want to receive. Gary Chapman, author of The Five Love Languages espouses five languages we each speak. Sometimes when we are speaking in our own language, we don't stop to consider our partner is speaking another language, hence breakdowns in communication. It's important to understand what language the other party also speaks so we can align our communication.

If we repurpose Chapman's five love languages for business, this may be the difference that makes the biggest difference in your business relationships. Do you know which of the following languages your client speaks? Do they want:

- **Quality Time** - Many of us appreciate quality time with our family and friends, so why wouldn't our prospects appreciate the same from us. We could ensure that we put in the time, research, preparation and value to our conversations, within the promised timeframes, and made our time together so worthwhile our potential buyer would think '*wow, that was a cool conversation.*'

- **Acts of Service** - This could be going above and beyond the call of duty when it comes to looking after extra things such as client deliveries or credit or administration issues to make them feel even more valued. The balance is to ensure your altruism is not detrimental to your business.

- **Gifts** - This could be as simple as sending information, white papers, a newsletter, a breakfast invitation or even publishing and sharing articles on social media to make your clients, or potential clients, feel they still mattered.

- **Words of Affirmation** - In the words of Dale Carnegie "People work for money but go the extra mile for recognition, praise and rewards". What that means for our buyer is that genuine validation, genuine compliments, professional recognition or a heartfelt '*thank you*' to let them know you truly care is all that may be needed.

- **Touch** - A little different in this politically correct world we live in today but how about making sure your handshakes aren't fierce grips or wet fish experiences to show you definitely respect them. For those of you with emotionally intelligent prospects or buyers, the rules are relaxing where bringing your whole self to work means being OK with a mutual hug.

Introducing words like 'love languages' into business is foreign in many cases. It's appearance on agendas could be disruptive and push boundary conditions, and seen as oh, so feminine in a masculine world, however, true connection, transparency and vulnerability is bringing a different level of awareness into the business world on a much needed basis, balancing out our conversations and relationships.

Energy Matters

In talking about love languages and feminine energy, where does that leave the masculine energy traits that form many current sales environments. Language that includes phrases such as, *'results only matter'*, *'stitch them up'*, or *'do a deal?'*, *'crush quota'* and the like?

Where are the balanced energy traits that include the softer skills of collaboration, caring and emotions? Those nurturing skills many of our customers really want so we make them feel special in return for their spending money with our business.

Medibank have recently been applauded for being the only Top 100 Company in Australia with more women than men on its Board, and not just to tick the gender equality box. According to Georgie Morell, "consumer driven companies must master the female psychology to survive and thrive as it will determine their fortunes and failures."

- Imagine if your business was so great at attracting potential clients and generated such huge demand that you didn't even need sellers.
- Imagine if your message to the market was so clear and so compelling that people flocked to buy from you. Where, like Kevin Costner in *'Fields of Dreams'*, you built it and they really did come.

- Imagine if you didn't measure your business purely by the profit you made but by the difference you made in the day to day working lives of the people you served, and that then rippled out to their family lives and the community.
- Imagine if your idea, product or service allowed your client to work smarter and more efficiently so they could leave work earlier to pick their kids up from school.
- Imagine if your buyer made such a great decision based on your guidance that they were able to generate more ways to grow their business and be promoted in the process.
- Imagine that you impacted your buyers spending in the right direction and they achieved their bonus as well as you achieving yours.

All because your intention had purpose. All because the meaning you put on your role was more than the almighty dollar and definitely more than your product or solution.

Would your customers love you? Would they send you testimonials and references and advocate for you without you asking? Would this energetic shift in positioning, thinking and selling make a difference? I think it just might!

How Relevant are You?

Today, it's all about measuring your relevance in the market through ideas you have for your customer's growth, in addition to the level of connection you have with your buyers. But more than that, it's about contribution - **to** your customers and **for** your customers, and the five word formula found in the intention of one simple question, *'How Can I Help You?'*

Just like anything in nature, if something is not growing and contributing, then it is dying. Business is no different. Business is a living organism and anyone who thinks different will die the death of a thousand extinct sellers. Just like Willy Loman in *'Death of a Salesman'*, if you aren't making change happen, developing personally, or being self motivated, people won't believe in you. It's not as simple as Willy thought, *"about being likeable through fakery, looking good, charming people and cracking jokes."* People know when you are faking it. People buy people. If you're not for real, they won't buy you. People want the real deal and the human element.

A great example of being human is the story that Tony Hsieh, CEO of Zappos, tells at the end of each of his presentations that he calls his *'pizza story.'* The story shares how Hsieh and some of his business partners were working into the night. Someone suggested that they grab some pizza, but everything was shut, and because they didn't know the area very well, tongue in cheek, Hsieh suggested they call Zappos. Sure enough, even though Zappos are not in the pizza business, the young girl who took the call found out where they were, asked what they wanted and arranged the nearest pizza joint to deliver the pizza.

Today, when you ask, *'How Can I Help You?'* you must be prepared to do whatever it takes, to be consistent and to walk your talk.

The Adventures of Hobbes

A story that was shared over sixty-five thousand times at last count on social media came from the experiences of a six-year-old boy and staff at an airport. The following is the excerpt from the Tampa Bay Times, written about their own local airport staff. *'The plane to*

Houston, Texas, had already left the gate when six-year-old Owen Lake
realized he'd left his favourite toy, a stuffed tiger named Hobbes, at the
airport in Tampa, Florida. The tiger was one of a kind, made by Owen's
grandmother to look like the one in the comic strip Calvin and Hobbes.
Owen's mother called Tampa International and discovered that the staff
didn't just rescue the lost tiger, but also took it on an adventure – taking
pictures of Hobbes' travels throughout the airport and made them into a
picture book for Owen.'

This is clearly a story of caring and helping and going the extra mile, which of course is a combination of love languages, masculine and feminine energy and doing whatever it takes.

What Business are You Really In?

Is the business world ready to move from the hard sell to the heart sell?

Selling needs to change, most of us know that. It needs to come back to basic courtesy and communication, respect and responsibility and serving those who make the decision to do business and pay to be served by us – both before the contract is signed as well as after the contract is signed.

So what business are you in? What business are you really in?

Zappos is definitely not in the pizza business and we would be forgiven for thinking they are in the shoe business, but ask Tony Hsieh and he will proudly tell you that they are in the business of selling happiness by delivering the best customer service.

Tampa Bay Airport and South West Airlines may be in the airline business but ask both and they would be proud to tell you they are more in the business of helping six year old boys feel very happy and giving people the freedom to fly.

As Dan Pink says, *'We are all in the business of moving people.'*

Fuji Xerox, for many years, was my home away from home and part of the growth and innovation the company and the people experienced was to reinvent the way we did business. Xerox redefined their message for us all and as sellers we naturally adapted and changed our message too. We no longer sold copiers, instead we helped our buyers adapt and innovate their businesses in order to *'transition their documents between the paper and digital worlds.'*

Kodak was another company I had a sales role in, but unfortunately they didn't make the shift in time. Had they realised the business they were really in was selling memories instead of yellow boxes of film, they might have made different decisions and not have had to file for bankruptcy.

Sales is not just the responsibility of the seller, but the responsibility of the whole organisation, from the production line to the front line. What difference could that make in the world of the buyer if everyone spoke the same language? If everyone collaborated, and forgot about the power they wielded in their own separate silos, if everyone realised that sales and protecting margin, reinvesting back into the business and contributing to the social fabric of society was all part of the bigger purpose. Imagine if the leader of a company educated the **whole company** on the virtues of selling. If everyone understood the words 'to sell' sprung from the Olde English word, Sellan, meaning 'to give'.

The Times They are A-Changin'

Clarity on the core values that define your role or your business is key. Do you have a CEO being measured on revenue and a sales manager in that same company being measured on profit? What conflicting messages are being sent to the troops? If this is the case, what ethical behaviours might that be creating? Or not creating!

More and more businesses are realising that whilst profits are important, so too, are values. Millennials are poised to make up 75% of the workforce by 2025 and are already favouring companies and businesses that work a triple bottom line of profits, people and planet. This shift, underpinned by purpose and values, is demonstrating that buyers are more likely to support companies that support all these parts, and on principle, they won't mind spending more money to do so. Clarity on the business you are in and the values that underpin the business is more important than ever.

As Bob Dylan sang in The Times they Are A Changing

Come mothers and fathers throughout the land
And don't criticize what you can't understand
Your sons and your daughters are beyond your command
Your old road is rapidly agin'
Please get out of the new one if you can't lend a hand
For the times they are a-changin'

The Value of Values

Leaders are slowly realising that purpose plays a large role in business today. The divide between the intention of sellers is becoming more noticeable because people are more in tune with what really matters. It is about values alignment.

The authors of 'Conscious Capitalism - Liberating the Heroic Spirit of Business', John Mackey and Raj Sisodia, outline the fact that in

1989, apart from the birth of the World Wide Web, the fall of the Berlin Wall and the massacre at Tianeman Square, for the first time in USA history, more than half of the population was over forty years of age. What that meant was that mid-life values were now beginning to drive change. People started to care. From a political, economic, technological, environmental and social perspective things began to shift. Even at a local community level, we began to see movements such as 'Quit Smoking', 'Slip Slop Slap' and 'Get into Life' campaigns filter into our psyche. People began to value the intangibles more than ever, including the purpose of their roles, businesses and industries.

The wellness industry today, is an example of this shift. Starting slowly only a few years ago, it is now worth $500 billion dollars, up nearly 50% in five years (Betterhealthworx). And it will double again to $1 trillion in the next five years. This is driven by a shift in values across all generations when it comes to food, beauty and health.

I believe we are on the cusp of change when it comes to the sales profession and that true intent to serve will redefine the way business is done. It will be helped along by the millennials and their voices as to what matters – in their role as both buyers and sellers.

People Don't Buy What, They Buy Why

When considering sustainability, Simon Sinek created a message and a movement with his Golden Circles. The what, the how and the power of why. However, whilst wonderfully simple, I believe these three Golden Circles are missing something fundamental – the real catalyst for change and sustainability, The Changemaker Circle.

For many of us, the space we play in begins at the outer circles where gaining clarity around the task at hand is key. The outer circle is the '**what**' - the KPI's, the numbers, the metrics. It's where we set goals and objectives and get really clear on our outcomes.

Next, we get clarity on '**how**' we get there. We brainstorm, we do trainings, we read and research and get all the left brain stuff happening. We do our reports, our to-do lists, our call plans and we stick with the processes as best we can.

And it's at this stage when many people stall, and even stop, in their quest to succeed. They have all the methodologies and structures and know the right things to say and do, but they never have the discipline and they fail to act. It's why sellers learn what to do but many never implement, execute, follow up or complete. Why is that?

As Sinek so eloquently phrases it, they don't have their purpose – their powerful '**why.**' He is right. But if sellers can't shift their own status quo, how on earth can they shift their buyers'? The main chokehold is their fear of change, regardless of how big their '**why**' is. We've all been there. We have all had a powerful purpose to create change in and around us, and yet something has stopped us in our tracks, even though our intention was so purposeful and profitable.

So What Prevents Real Success?

Recently I sat in a boardroom with a respected sales director and we discussed his team's performance and lack of performance, and what needed to change. We talked KPI's and milestones, tactics and strategies and as the conversation got deeper, he proudly and passionately pointed to a framed print on the wall showing his company's powerful *corporate why*, defined in one short, succinct sentence. It was certainly crystal clear and compelling, and then the conversation stopped. It was almost as though the boxes had all been ticked with this purposeful message, and they would set the world on fire. They weren't, so I asked him some tough questions:

- Who do your team need to become individually, to collectively live that *why?*
- Who are the customers you have who will appreciate that particular *why?*
- Who are your customers buying in this *Connection Economy* – your people or the competition?'

The importance of understanding and executing the 'who' is not just limited to the world of sellers. Award winning actress, Reece Witherspoon, on addressing her fear of speaking in front of an audience (acting on screen is apparently totally different than speaking in front of a live audience) shared, *"Because of this experience, I know that if I want to do things that matter, I need to get comfortable with being uncomfortable. I worked through my fear because I put myself in a difficult situation over and over again until my anxiety subsided."* Whilst she had her powerful *why* she needed to address a deeper level to truly succeed. That level was 'who' she needed to become to achieve her dream.

Sinek's famous phrase, *"People don't buy what you do, they buy why you do it"* may be very true in business, but to share that *why* in a compelling commercial manner, the person sharing it has to have a real level of conviction, the ability to share the message in a commercial and relevant context and they must have an intention to truly contribute to the buyer and their business growth. They need to own their own value and bring that value to the table for the benefit of all. More importantly, *'people don't buy what you do, they buy what they want to do, who they are and who they want to be!'*

The Missing Circle

I believe, the **who** is the missing circle in Simon's Sinek's Golden Circles model.

The Wright Brothers succeeded in selling their crazy, awesome dream, not just because of their *why* but because they were prepared to be **who they needed to be** and do what it took to live their *why*. Their supportive home life gave them a strong sense of self belief, which in time allowed them to stand up against the theories of more experienced aeronautical experiments. To choose not to marry so they could live their purpose and make the world a more connected place says a lot about **who they were and who they were prepared to not be**. Their sense of resilience and confidence enabled them to keep on going when they were faced with sceptics, critics and nay-sayers, and their resourcefulness stood them in good stead when failure struck, as it did again and again. It is not dissimilar to the environment sellers and business leaders find themselves in today.

Who you are speaks louder than what you do or why you do it!

This chapter has been about the bigger conversations, the conversations many people don't stop to contemplate or consider — especially in the cut and thrust world of selling.

This book is about it being your turn to make a difference and to not just become a modern day seller, but a connected and contributing human being who stands in their god given power.

THE MODERN DAY SALESPERSON

REFLECTING ON THE words of one of the world's greatest salesmen, the late Steve Jobs, he addressed the students at Stanford in his commencement speech in 2005 on the topic of who you need to be: *'You have to trust in something, your gut, destiny, life, karma, whatever, because believing that the dots will connect down the road will give you the confidence to follow your heart, even when it leads you off the well-worn path, and that will make all the difference.'*

And not to drive home too fine a point in cementing the power of **'who'**, was demonstrated by one of our modern day saleswomen, JK Rowling. Her *Harry Potter Series* of books have gained worldwide attention; they have won multiple awards, and become the best-selling book series in history, having sold more than four hundred million copies. She shared in her speech to the graduates of Harvard in 2008, *"One of the many things I learned at the end of that Classics corridor down which I ventured at the age of 18, in search of something I could not then define, was this, written by the Greek author Plutarch: 'What we achieve inwardly will change outer reality'. That is an astonishing statement and yet proven a thousand times every day of our lives. It expresses, in part,* *our inescapable connection with the outside world, the fact that we touch other people's lives simply by existing."*

Who we are matters. Who we are is what we buy when we buy anything. Who we are is also what our buyers buy.

The Changemaker Circles

To create real long term and sustainable change is to start with the outside circles of defining '**what**' we need to do. With a learning mindset we learn '**how**' to do it. We get clear on '**why**' it is necessary to execute, and ultimately we must look at '**who**' we need to be to complete it. When we know who we  need to be, we show up differently. It becomes so much easier and effortless for us to move up and back out of the circles living our '**why**', doing what we know '**how**' and achieving '**what**' we set as outcomes.

The new breed of seller needs to be able to work within all four circles and leverage both their available external resources such as technology, tools, equipment or people, as well as access their internal resourcefulness, such as resilience, courage or commitment to be even more effective.

This book commercialises the Changemaker Circles by identifying and focusing on *the art of commercial conversations* relevant to the role of a seller today, underpinned by the Leadership Triad.

The Foundation - The Leadership Triad

The three categories that form the Leadership Triad, when developed even more, align the seller to today's buyer in an extremely empowering way.

POSITION! Personal Leadership - The Value of Self

Clearly our **positioning** and approach that we led with in the past is not as effective today as it once was. We have so many options open to us today, including a cross section of buyers and decision makers spanning multiple generations from Millennials to Baby Boomers. This means we've got to be able to meet the buyer where they are – whether that is online or offline, and adjust our style to suit them. We need to redefine the ABC's of selling from *'Always Be Closing'* through *'Always Be Connecting'* to *'Always Be Contributing.'*

We need to make our buyers curious enough about us to contact us when researching potential suppliers. We need to stand out from the very beginning and not be vanilla, beige or insignificant, namely not get lost amongst our competitors. In order to do so we need to own who we are, believe that the first sale must always be made to ourselves and approach our buyer with total conviction. It's about so much more than contacting them in order to convince them to buy our product. Rather, it's to be a magnet so they partner with us, and only us.

THINK! Thought Leadership –The Value of Your Offering

We know the sales conversation has been completely turned on its head, as has the buying process. As a result, we need to completely recalibrate our **thought process** and focus of our conversations. We need to do more than walk in the buyers' shoes and be empathetic. We need to know what shoes they wear and buy the same pair. We need to get on the same side of the table as the buyer more than ever before and to do that we need to shift our questions to ones with depth and breadth and significantly elevate our care factor. We also need to know what makes us unique and be able to deliver that message to the market in a strong commercial manner.

Learning how to redefine and position our offering in a more relevant, tailored and contextual way includes changing our questions, our statements and the way we think.

SELL! Sales Leadership and Your Value to the Market

An intention to serve, to collaborate and to contribute to a client's business is what the profession of **selling** is all about. It is about outcomes and dynamics where everyone wins. Businesses with this intention and conscious approach will attract and retain those people who buy into their mission – staff and customers alike. With staff loyalty and talent retention being such an issue for businesses today, living the values in 'real time' means the sales profession will be viewed as contributors, as givers and as the good guys – and girls! Their care factor will show up in conversations, negotiations and relationships through conversations that equate to a, *'How Can I Help You?'* mindset, creating and providing both purpose and profits.

Welcome to *The Art of Commercial Conversations*

History has dealt us the science and the mechanics behind selling. I believe it is time to view selling through more of the lens that encourages it as an art, so we can begin to paint a different commercial landscape.

This book offers a philosophy around the shift necessary in the minds and hearts of those who go out day after day to share a message and make a difference, whether they are sellers, sales leaders or business owners.

Whilst it is not designed as a linear 'how to' book, it does provide prescriptions to some challenges and implementable ideas to activate your results immediately. Throughout the book we have generically referred to all business people who have a responsibility to generate revenue, as *sellers*. Each chapter matches a current business shift, a seller's thinking and the importance of the art behind that conversation.

Woven through the fabric of the nine commercial conversations are reminders from the Changemaker Circles:

- What you need to do
- How you do it
- Why you do it and
- Who you need to be to succeed

It is important to note that we cannot, and will not, negate the transactional seller, because we all need to know those basic skills. Nor we are not going to dismiss the transitional, relationship seller even though The Challenger Sale refers to only 7% of successful sellers being relationship driven. It is my belief that we need **all** these skills in order to bring our whole self to market.

We have also introduced a different way of thinking to give clarity on what our buyers want from us. This allows us to buy into their expectations and remain relevant in our market place.

As sellers, we are each on our own journey and that includes stepping up to the plate with conviction, having those conversations that not only drive value but are driven by purposeful values and in the right business context. Most importantly, it is also to contribute to our business and our customers business and to be even more mindful of the ripple effect and impact we have on the wider community.

Let's begin with Book One – how we **POSITION** ourselves in order to have our commercial conversations (our personal leadership). Let's explore Book Two and consider our conversations based on how we **THINK** and how we develop our dialogue with the buyer (our thought leadership). Finally, let's complete our learning by addressing the conversations that will deliver our value driven outcomes by way of our style and how we **SELL,** in Book Three.

'When you sell with heart, you don't treat clients like transactions.'

Linda Richardson

A MANIFESTO FOR CONSCIOUS SELLERS

CONVICTION - The Art of Rebellion - It's more than loving what we do. It's having the courage to be seen, to take our turn, to change our rules, to step outside our fears and love what we bring to the table.

CONNECT - The Art of Mindfulness - It's more than kumbaya and yogis. It's the opportunity to centre ourselves in a busy and noisy world so we can stand grounded and confident and be present to our buyer.

CONTACT - The Art of Social - It's about BEING social, not just being ON social. It's more than a playground where we go to play, it's like being in an auditorium where we can team up, play our hearts out and be seen by those who will see our value.

CONTENT - The Art of Story - It's more than features, advantages and benefits. It's the ability to tell a story that captivates and spread that story to the world through messages that create value.

CONSULT - The Art of Tension - It's more than asking questions. It's creating a space to get personal, to be bold, to push the boundaries for all the right reasons and to create change in our clients' worlds.

CONTEXT - The Art of Meaning - It's not about what you think it's about. Its essence is in interpretation, variation, listening for understanding and being prepared to get it wrong.

CONTRACT - The Art of The Ask - It's not about closing the deal. It's about learning to say *yes* and learning to say *no* and understanding the magic that happens in between.

CONVERSE - The Art of Conspiracy - It's not about keeping in touch, customer service or moments of truth. It's about working together, joint ventures and collaboration.

CONTRIBUTE - The Art of The Start - It's not about the money or the profits or shareholders. It's about the meaning and the purpose and the stakeholders.

BOOK ONE

POSITION!

THE VALUE OF YOU
AND YOUR
PERSONAL LEADERSHIP

CONVICTION

THE ART OF REBELLION

*It's more than loving what we do. It's having the courage
to be seen, to take our turn, to change our rules, to step
outside our fears and love what we bring to the table.*

THE MEANING OF the word conviction has its deep-seated roots around rules. It conjures up images of people being punished, imprisoned and exiled for breaking the rules of society.

Right now, we need to start breaking some of the old rules because the game of selling is being rewritten and what worked in the past just won't work today.

Results may not be as dramatic as having a formal conviction handed down to us by judge and jury, but at times it may seem like it. Through conditioning, fear and a mindset of lack, it is so easy to lock ourselves into our own confined corner and not see the abundant opportunities, true potential and rewards that are available. The rules we have imposed on ourselves, more so than anything else, are what we need to break.

Rules are being broken in all areas of society today to allow change to happen - it's called innovation, progression and growth.

We see religion loosening its grip on rules, freshening up the leadership, introducing modern day shifts that are all inclusive with the changing of the guard and the introduction of a new Pope.

We see education freeing up their old ways and introducing student-based curriculum at local schools, or online universities appearing such as the Khan University for global students. In doing so, **all** learning styles are being recognised, instead of authoritative based regulations that dictated only one right way where so many students were, and still are, disadvantaged.

We see the real estate market being disrupted with the likes of unique consumer focussed funding models targeted at giving the consumer control of the sale through more choice rather than antiquated percentage models.

We see business changing where the focus is not only on *getting the numbers* but on the introduction of heart, vulnerability and authenticity in parallel with hard core results and accountability, and not just the latter in isolation.

We see society changing and embracing diversity of all kinds. With the recent gay marriage bill passed in Australia, albeit a lagging decision, rules are being broken. In addition, the focus on bringing more women into the heavily populated alpha male domain of sales, albeit a cause unto itself, the needle is moving in the right direction.

Re-Imagining the Future

The world is changing, and the status quo is being reimagined. Fear and a *'lack mindset'* are being highlighted as reasons for stagnation and failure. The one way to address fear and lack in business development is to introduce its antithesis and that is love and abundance, but who wants to speak of love and abundance in business? Why wouldn't you though when it revolves around a mindset that says there is enough for everyone. We don't need to discount, we don't need to badmouth the competition, and we don't need to be greedy wolves of any street!

To have conviction in yourself and what you stand for, to be able to back yourself regardless of what is in front of you, is to have courage. And courage is all about having a full heart, embracing your fears and realising you, and what you bring to the table, will benefit yourself and others, even more.

When Dorothy walked through Oz and came across the tinman, the lion and the scarecrow on her path, we know it was a metaphor for what was already buried deep within her - intelligence, courage and heart. Filled with her new-found conviction, she clicked her ruby red shoes and found herself back in Kansas ready to make more decisions, face more fears and act out more choices. We all have a Dorothy inside us and we are already wearing those shoes that will take us to wherever we want to go. We don't need to only stand in our customers' shoes as we have been advised to do for so long, we need to change the rules and stand strong and tall in our own shoes.

For the modern-day seller to make the shift from an environment of caveat emptor (let the customer beware) to caveat venditor (let the seller beware), or from a world of lack thinking to one of abundance, then the seller must do more than constantly convince buyers that their solution is the best.

They must have conviction in what they do and must demonstrate intelligence, courage and heart in a market that is slowly waking up and realising the importance of a well rounded, win/win/win approach, focus and outcome as opposed to the old world of winner take all. They realise it's time that they donned their leadership capes and set out to change their worlds and their buyers' worlds. It's about disrupting the status quo and selling change!

When making that first sale to yourself you rewrite the rules. You stand strong in the conviction that what you believe in, and what you are selling, is a solid foundation for contributing to your buyer's business growth.

Imagine if your intent was to always sell change. That to grow your business was based on having to make change happen in your customer's business. What difference might that make in your approach? How would you measure it? Selling with a product only based mindset is not enough.

But not enough sellers will break their own personal rules because they have stories that drive them. Stories that are hidden. Stories that serve them and give their excuses, blaming and self-sabotaging behaviours some form of weird credence.

According to Dave Kurlan from the Objective Management Group and the extensive research he has done across thousands of sellers over countless years, there are five hidden weaknesses all sellers have in varying degrees that prevents a seller or a business from generating the revenue that is so available to them.

- The need for approval where being the buyer's friend and being liked is more important than asking the questions that will qualify the buyer as an opportunity or not.
- They believe the buyer and whether people agree or not, sometimes buyers can be liars. Asking qualifying questions and not taking what they say on face value is difficult for some sellers, but will go a long way to changing the *'I'll get back to you'* responses many buyers use.
- Their money beliefs will prevent them asking questions related to money, budgets or financials, which are a key part of any commercial conversation, because they don't feel comfortable.
- A non-supportive buy cycle means how you buy will dictate what answers you will accept or not accept from your buyer. If they will think about the purchase and your style is to think things over too, then you will empathise a little too much and accept their response.
- The propensity to become emotional means you let the voices in your head override your ability to maintain a sales process that ensures you control your own conversation.
- The ability to not just face rejection but handle it is not so cut and dried. We all know that sellers have a fear of rejection and when you realise that rejection actually impacts the same part of the brain that reacts to physical pain, will go part the way to understanding the psyche of the seller. Overcoming rejection is more about how long you take to get over whatever it is that caused you to feel that way. Do you go for a walk after some form of rejection or do you take a week to pick up the phone again?

These are five examples of where your rules may need to be broken and rewritten.

The Impact of Cause and Effect

Most sellers, though, won't break their rules, shift their status quo or embrace unfamiliarity because of their version of cause and effect and what doing so will mean to them. If I do (x) then (y) will happen. It's easier to stagnate, play victim, make excuses, blame and feel hopeless. Their rules rule them.

- If I leave a message and no one rings me back, it means a) they don't want to talk to me, b) they don't like me, c) I've failed, or in some cases all three.
- If I up sell or cross sell after they have made an enquiry, then I am taking more money off them rather than realising the benefit their business will receive by buying more from me.
- If I try to speak to the CXO Level and they say *no*, then what value do I really have to offer if I can't even get an appointment? I'm not enough, so I'll either retreat or leave those conversations to my manager.
- If I start posting content on social media, what if it's not perfect and people negate it, what if they disagree and end up judging me? So, it's easier to sit back and watch others, critique them and stay beige instead.

If... then...

How many rules do you have that prevent you moving forward? Rules based on old stories which no longer serve you. Rules that mean you stay in your own fear based and fixed mindset and never grow.

What Must Have to Happen?

Do you know the rules you are operating by? To find out your own rules is to ask yourself the following question: *What must have to happen?*

- 'What must have to happen for someone to call me back?'
- 'What must have to happen for me to respond to an objection?'
- 'What must have to happen for me to know I have value to offer a CXO contact?'
- 'What must have to happen for me to confidently share my ideas?'

What are your answers? Are they completely unrealistic or ridiculous? Then it's your choice and chance to change them.

Most rules are operating past their use by date and need a complete overhaul. To change the way you think, is to be aware of your condition beliefs and understand the emotional states, or values, that are important to you. It is then to identify the rules that must happen to meet those values. As an example, here are some values and corresponding rules elicited from a few of my clients:

- What must have to happen for you to feel the value of success? Is it to make 150% of target every single month, or make an appointment with every single contact you make? Are those rules serving or sabotaging your results? Do those rules need to be loosened or tightened a little?

- What must have to happen for you to feel the value of acceptance? Ahhh... your customer must call you back in 24 hours? Really? Is that your rule or your buyer's? What if you knew **their** rules were to respond within 3 days? Would that change how you think?

- What must have to happen for you to experience the value of intelligence? Is it to press that *publish* button on LinkedIn and share your own thoughts and ideas to help your audience? Is what's stopping you the fact that you need more depth or knowledge? Or that your English teacher from Grade Six who said you would never be able to string two sentences together, might just be reading it?

Many sellers will say that one of the most important emotional states, or *'toward values'* they have is *'success'*, yet another one of their most important emotional states, or *'away from values'*, is that they never want to experience *'rejection.'*

If human nature tells us that every human being will do more to avoid pain than gain pleasure, that means they will do more to avoid rejection than achieve success. Because what we focus on is what we get. If we focus on not wanting to be rejected, then we will do everything in our power to prevent that happening. This is the exact reason why sellers have call reluctance, never ask for the order, discount at the drop of a hat and are happy to hang out with the people who don't make the decisions or negotiate. Their values are in conflict, and it's the internal dialogue and rules that drives it.

This prevents a seller from being in the moment or being present to a conversation with the buyer. If the buyer is not giving anything away, not responding the way you want, appearing rude, busy, reacting with no energy, then the seller goes inside their head and the incessant inner voice starts playing. *'This is new – but do I have to ask a different question? If I ask a different question, what if they don't know what I mean, what if I don't even know what I mean? OMG! What did that pause mean, that look– people don't do that if they are 'into' you... how am I ever going to influence them if I don't know what already influences them? I won't be enough if I am real, if I am myself, if I show them the vulnerable side of me, do I really have to shift my beliefs around money and my need for being liked and, and, and?'* How exhausting!

Research has shown that this level of fear and perfectionism and holding onto rules so tightly, not only stops us from being successful, it increases our stress levels leading to anxiety and depression. It emotionally, mentally and sometimes physically, imprisons us. And because the sales landscape now is made up of budgets blowing out, it being harder to connect with people and margins being squeezed, then stress levels definitely are increasing (up to 60% according to 2000 sellers surveyed by salesdog.com). It's up to us to lower these levels even more. It's up to us to own our value, stand in certainty, and back ourselves more than ever.

To change your thinking in order to serve you and help you stand in your conviction is as simple as deciding to decide. To help you, let me ask you one very powerful question:

> *'If you didn't have those excuses or rules that you run your business and life with, what would you do differently and how would achieving your outcome be easier?'*

Be Seen

Being you is so important to you and everyone else. Being the real deal is so important to your buyer. *"Authenticity is a practice – something you choose every day."* Brene Brown says. It is the practice, she says, of asking yourself: *"Am I going to show up and let myself be seen?"*

The facts of life are not the birds and the bees. The facts of life are that half the people you meet and know will disapprove of something about you – how you open a conversation, the way you dress, where you live, the company you work for, the accent you speak with, the colour of your skin, the success you achieve….ad infinitum.

Being seen is letting perfectionism go. Being seen is more than believing in the value you offer. It's a knowing. Being seen is losing the attachment to what other people think. There is no such thing as perfection, so I don't even know why the word was invented, except to create internal prisons for people who live in that make-believe world. Don't worry about people liking you or being like you.

It's this fear driven dialogue that kills the ability for **you** to be **you**, and yet our customers are telling us they want **you** – not some canned version of you. They want someone who can sit with them or present to them and package up some awesome insights and deliver in a way that is transparent. They want someone to challenge their thinking, to be seen as the go-to person and to give them *aha* moments they can build upon. They want nothing more than to be sitting at the traffic lights in a moment of reflection a week later, thinking 'That was a cool idea – how can I make it happen?' What they don't want is... a seller peddling a product or service.

I am not going to Dr Phil you or ask you to lie on a couch and dig into the meaning of what happened when you were five years of age that is causing you to sabotage yourself as an adult. I am going to ask you to consider what your buyers might be thinking: *'Who are you? How much do you care about me and why should I care about you?'*

It's the transformational and inspiring sellers who operate from a state of conviction and belief in what they are doing and who know why they are doing it. It is the transformational and inspiring sellers who are able to lift the conversation to a new level of relevance and meaning, and who have an outcome based on more than signing the contract, rather contributing to the customer's business.

In the new world, building your levels of conviction is not a hard skills training. The brain, the thinking, the language and the behaviour all need to morph and work together to design an authentic connection. In order to influence other people, you need to know what influences them in the first place – and to achieve that you need to know what influences **you**.

To convince someone to buy means there will be very little connection. In many cases people may buy because there is no alternative, or they don't want, or need, a connection because a transaction is enough. In most other cases, though, where there is no connection, there will be no trust. Where there is no trust you will most likely lose that opportunity you hoped for, miss out on the positive feedback or dip out on a referral - and not even know why!

When you come from a space of conviction, however, it is different. You own the value of you, your product and your company. There is an energy that is hard to resist. Both you and your offer become attractive and compelling. You are pulled toward the sale by your buyer, rather than you having to push your product and solution onto the buyer. This is why it is so important to understand not just you, but your buyer, their process and their psyche, and to connect with them on a human level.

So how do you create a state of conviction? How do you learn to step out and really back yourself? How do you get seen? How do you know what influences others to give you that confidence?

What Influences Every Single One of Us?

We all have a human need for certainty, staying safe and not wanting to venture too far out into an area that leaves us vulnerable. But on the other hand, we also get to a point where we know we have to step out and do something different. We might feel bored and decide on a little uncertainty and risk. We might feel under pressure to do something different or we might feel guilty enough to be catapulted into taking some out of the ordinary action.

Whatever it might be, entering into a world of uncertainty is also one of our human needs. Paradoxically, we need both certainty and uncertainty. Give us too much uncertainty though, and we will quickly head back to the land of predictability. Give us too much sameness and we search for different.

This shows up in sellers when it comes to call reluctance, lack of administrative responsibility and procrastination. They may have a burst of energy, success, rejection or activity that moves them in that moment. They'll live in that space for a while and then by their nature, they slip into complacency, mediocrity or procrastination again, meeting that need for certainty in an unresourceful way.

To stand in our conviction, we really need to meet our need for certainty in a strong, resourceful way and that means embracing uncertainty and all the fears, doubts and apprehensions that come with it. It's about consistently staring down the face of uncertainty, and saying, *'Bring it! I'm ready!'*

And when you have that outlook on life you really can do anything. Change will happen in you and around you quite effortlessly.

Maslow had a theory about the hierarchy of human needs and it included five needs, Physiological, Safety, Social, Esteem and Self Actualisation. Anthony Robbins expanded on that to create the Six Core Human Needs model around why we do what we do and what influences us all.

The Six Core Needs are like our engine room with **everything** we think or do being the vehicles that allow us to meet these six needs. The first four needs are the needs of our personality. Everything we do, or think, will meet these needs resourcefully or unresourcefully. The final two needs are the needs of the spirit and include growth and contribution. Two factors that are lacking in many sellers. When we meet all six of these needs in a resourceful way, it's because we love what we do, feel confident and are totally fulfilled.

Physical or personal needs	Certainty	⟷	Variety
	Significance	⟷	Connection
Spiritual needs	Growth	⟷	Contribution

What are the Six Core Human Needs?

- **Certainty** -We all have a need for certainty, where we need to feel sure about things, we need to feel safe in our environment and secure in our world. It is our need to avoid pain and gain pleasure.

- **Uncertainty** - When we are satiated with too much certainty, predictability or sameness, then we seek variety. Paradoxically, we will look for uncertainty, risk or adventure in our life to counterbalance the certainty, the predictability or the boredom of staying safe.

- **Significance** –We also have a need for significance and to feel special or good enough. It depends on whether we meet that need for significance in a healthy or unhealthy way. Blaming the economy or whinging about pricing is a vehicle for meeting the need for significance unresourcefully. Competing with a peer in a sales competition or doing something to help someone will meet that same need in a resourceful way.

- **Connection** - We all have a need for connection in our lives, whether it is connection with our clients, colleagues or ourselves. We repel connection with others though if our levels of significance are unresourcefully high. I'm sure we all know someone who has made us feel worse after meeting them; the ones who craves recognition in a self serving way; the one who talks about themselves all the time, or worse still, negatively about others. They usually have difficulty connecting with others. People are polite to them but also prefer to keep their distance.

- **Growth** - Like anything in nature, you must grow or ... die! If someone does not have a growth mindset then their mindset and approach is referred to as fixed, and with agility being a key criterion in business today, a fixed mindset is dangerous.

- **Contribution** - Finally, we all have a need to contribute, to give more than ourselves, which is why we feel great when we help someone else; when we share or put a smile on someone's face or when we know we've made a difference.

To put this into perspective, let's look at two different scenarios involving sellers. One demonstrates the growth mindset and the thinking of a seller who is consistently successful. The other involves the fixed mindset and thinking behind a seller who is consistently unsuccessful. Can you see yourself or someone you know in these scenarios?

THE SELLER WHO IS CONSISTENTLY SUCCESSFUL

The seller who continually backs himself, knows he can sell, has a healthy self esteem, has certainty about his time management, his ethics and his intentions, meets his need for **certainty** at a high level and in an empowering way.

He also meets his needs for **uncertainty**, variety or risk at a resourceful level when he puts himself in a situation that may be unfamiliar, nerve wracking and risky, such as launching new campaigns or risking rejection from a referral or follow up.

He takes himself lightly and gets a thrill through the continuing challenge of winning the business, or simply through a variety of contacts he has that make his life interesting. By meeting his need for **significance** at a high level, he feels good about his decisions, knows he has helped his customer, moves out of his comfort zone and recognises little wins along the way.

He has high personal leadership skills, volunteers to help and speaks up for himself and others. His need for **connection** is met by supporting others, being a friend, listening, connecting regularly with his manager and his customers and therefore being totally resourceful.

If we were to consider the need for **growth**, he will ensure every interaction will teach him something, as will every loss he may experience, providing him with feedback and growth. He continues to be on top of his industry research and administrative responsibilities.

Meeting all of these needs combined provides on-going growth and improvement and as a result he can **contribute** to the business, the customer and his own environment positively. This seller would consider himself fulfilled in his role.

THE SELLER WHO IS NOT CONSISTENTLY SUCCESSFUL

This seller meets his need for **certainty** and stability in an unresourceful way because he doesn't back himself at all, has a fear of picking up the phone and is intimated when speaking to the decision maker. He doesn't do anything until it is 100% correct or risk free, so ends up procrastinating and keeping himself safe.

As a result of this self-imposed perfectionism he never reaches his standards, which realistically means he has no standards to speak of. His need for **uncertainty** and variety is met through constant overwhelm and he will tend to self sabotage in order to create some drama in his life and give him something different to focus on.

He chats to customers who can't make decisions, yet are happy to spend time with him, thereby making him feel important. This meets his need for **significance** at a high level, due to the attention he receives, albeit unresourceful attention.

His significance is also met by his victim mentality, be it blaming, whinging or making excuses about the economy, price or pay structure.

Because of this behaviour, connecting with the decision maker is limited and with his sales manager, it is low. He will tend to be needy, have unhealthy relationships and **connect** through problems rather than people.

If we consider how this seller meets his need for **growth**, it is nonexistent. Learning, upskilling and sharpening the axe is not on his radar. As a result, meeting his need for **contribution** to others and the business is also nonexistent.

This seller will more than likely not feel fulfilled or successful in his role and therefore won't last because he is not meeting any of his six needs at a resourceful level.

Both personas think and act the way they do because their thoughts and actions are meeting their human needs. There is a payoff for each of them at some level.

Our customers are no different and their reactions to us and how we position ourselves also have to tick the same six boxes. Their needs are met, or not met, through their conversations with us. Can you perhaps see yourself as a buyer in the following scenarios? Or maybe you can notice similar patterns in a prospective buyer or existing customer.

- The buyer who procrastinates and doesn't decide, may be doing so because it meets his need for certainty, while the buyer who is stressed out will more than likely also be meeting his need for certainty and control.
- The buyer who wants to have his name on everything or be the one to take the proposal to the Board, will more than likely be meeting his need for significance.
- The buyer that wants to chat all day long has a strong need for connection, while the buyer who is keen to put in the newest equipment is not just meeting his need for significance, but uncertainty, risk and variety as well.

Once you understand what your own top two personal human needs are and what influences you, then you are in a stronger position to know what drives and influences others. That gives you the ability to direct your discussions, questions and behaviour around that insight, and meet their needs at a subconscious level.

The First Sale is Always to Yourself

If we realise our clients want to see us as leaders, as trusted advisors, as true thought leaders, respected industry resources or changemakers, then we must rebel against our old stories. We must operate from a baseline of courage and conviction and sell with heart. If we want to approach our clients with total conviction then we need to start with ourselves and buy into that conviction of who we are, what we sell, the brand we represent as well as how we really show up. How do you show up?

By digging a little deeper and peeling back the curtain on your traits even more and by identifying the areas that are holding you back, it's a great opportunity to create a new story about who and what you are capable of being, doing and having and to connect more fully with those around you.

To take your levels of conviction to the next level and connect with others more effectively, then turn the pages. But first, a little reflection time....

SELF REFLECTION

- What has been the biggest rule you have holding you back in connecting with key people and generating more sales?

....
....
....

- How would you like the future to be different and what is important about that to you?

....
....
....

- What are you trying to prove by sabotaging yourself with made up stories and illusions that are only true in your mind?

....
....
....

- What human needs are they meeting?

....
....
....

- What must have to happen to position yourself with more conviction?

....
....
....

"I do know that the right words, spoken from the heart with conviction, with a vision of a better place and a faith in the unseen, are a call to action"

Deval Patrick

CONNECT

THE ART OF MINDFULNESS

It's more than kumbaya and yogis. It's the opportunity to centre ourselves in a busy and noisy world so we can stand grounded and confident and be present to our buyer.

CONNECTION IS LIKE plugging into a relationship with someone and flicking the switch. Energy flows and the lights go on. For any relationship to be extremely effective it's about creating this spark through genuine care, authentic interest, curiosity and sharing. Many sellers create a baseline level of superficial support and connection to just-do-what-they-have-to-do to do the job. Because buyers today want *'real'* and they want energy and ideas and connection, then not caring is risky business.

In sales training of old, we used to be encouraged to look for anything to build that rapport and connect at any level – golf clubs in the corner, photos on desks, and awards on walls, anything that we could use as rapport. I vividly remember securing an appointment with a very senior executive of a university, a Pro-Vice Chancellor to be exact. Walking into his office on the first appointment, I scoured his office for something, looking for anything that I could latch onto and leverage in order to connect with him.

There on his credenza, was a photo of him with his arm around a celebrity Australian Rules football player, Dermot Brereton who was a key player for the Hawthorn Football Club at the time. You have to imagine the hair fashion in the 1980's and the fact that Brereton had a mullet - long blonde, curly permed hair.

So, in a flippant manner, leveraging on the fact that my husband and kids barracked for Hawthorn, I continued my rapport building by stating, 'My husband would kill to have his photo taken with Dermot Brereton.'

This buyer looked at me.... Looked at the photo...., looked back at me and proceeded to tell me it was his wife!

It's great to be remembered! But for the right reasons! Selling in the 21st century is about connecting but definitely not by getting up front and personal too quickly. That can be quite awkward! Trust me!!!

So, what are the steps to connecting in a genuine and everyday way?

Our Initial Judgements

Statistics tell us that first impressions count and in the first couple of seconds we make a judgement on everyone we meet, consciously or subconsciously, and then spend a little longer checking in with ourselves that we have, in fact, made the right judgement.

If we were to walk down a narrow street on the wrong side of town and see a guy with tattoos, shaved head and rolling around drunk, most people would make a first impression that would see them cross to the opposite side of the road. Similarly, if we saw a couple of nuns, dressed in their habits, swinging their rosary beads in that same narrow street, we'd feel quite comfortable because what we perceived they represented would make us feel safe. We would more than likely smile back.

We make assumptions, or judgements, or perceptions based on our human need to feel safe, our need for certainty. This is because our brain distrusts different. It will default to shut down if it perceives we are in danger. And that danger can be as simple as meeting a buyer for the first time. Not knowing what to say. Feeling intimidated. Thinking you don't know enough. We've all experienced those moments.

What happens? The 'thinking part' of the brain shuts down. Your mind goes blank. You don't stay in the moment. You second guess. You let them lead. You forget to ask key questions.

Why? Because, like any electrical device, the brain goes on standby – and remember the brain is a total electrical device. All your body needs to make it function when it goes into a flight or fight or freeze scenario is for the blood to pump, the muscles to work, the lungs to breathe and the heart to beat. The rest of your brain is not needed. So, on a sales call, as a seller, when your body freezes, your heart beats at a million miles an hour, your muscles tense up and your breathing quickens because you are nervous or lack confidence. You are in survival mode.

Our customer's brains do the same to protect them, as well. They also form their own opinions and perceptions of us and they go into survival mode when they feel any form of threat or tension. If you were to ask a buyer to describe a salesperson in one or two words, let's just say it wouldn't be complimentary. Therefore, due to stereotypical role perceptions, it's only human nature that the buyer would feel some type of 'threat' and therefore they would be cautious.

At a conscious level there are many ways we've been taught to shortcut this reaction by manoeuvring a few things:

- We can learn the ways to match and mirror our clients by being aware of their body language, their breathing, their tonality and naturally align and leverage what we have in common. When we are in rapport, mirror neurons in the brain will naturally mirror the behaviour of the person in front of us and we become truly empathetic – we feel chemistry, or we are in sync with that person and trust is built. If there is no natural rapport, then you are able to manipulate the situation by 'mirroring and matching'. In other words, mimicking the other person to build greater trust. One point to remember is that our buyers BS meters will pick that behaviour up in a heartbeat and we don't advise it.

- We can also pick the type of person they are in the first two or three sentences if we listen to how they speak. If they are fast talkers. We talk fast. If they are laid back, then we act laid back, if they dress casually, then turning up in a three-piece suit would send a signal that says, 'he is not like me'. The brain distrusts different.

- We can determine their personalities and find out whether they are a driver who knows what they want, an interactive who enjoys a chat, a steadfast who is conscious of the relationship status or a cautious person who wants to tick the boxes and adjust our initial approach so they think, 'he is like me'. It's being on their level or being aligned to their style.

Staying in Sync

When I kick-start the day at my group boot camp, I want to be like everyone there. I want to keep up with the group jogging, so I match their speed and flow. As a group, we are in sync; we have a pattern and a rhythm going. We pace each other until someone decides it's time to up the ante and run out front, and what do we all do? Because we are in flow, in sync, in rapport – we naturally follow each other.

Rapport is a state of trust and responsiveness *'in the moment.'* Contrary to many seller's beliefs, our buyers are not looking for a best friend. Most buyers are aware of the purpose and need for rapport and then expect to get down to business. To create rapport is business etiquette.

To have rapport work for you, you must believe you are enough. You also have got to want to truly connect with that person with an intention of creating value. You've got to realise that your buyer has a BS meter that sorts the wheat from the chaff pretty quickly, and the sorting criteria is not usually based on price. It is based on the genuine vibes they feel from you and the genuine value they can sense you will give both their business and them professionally.

It's More Than Rapport

At the end of the day connection is about more than building rapport. It's about caring and sharing and dreaming big. It's about being human. The lines between business and personal are beginning to merge these days as a direct result of technology providing more and more transparency. People don't want two dimensional relationships; they want to see more of who you are and will look for that when researching you and doing their due diligence.

For things to be real and authentic and for there to be a genuine connection with a buyer, team mate or leader, it's about having the emotional intelligence to connect with yourself first. To have an awareness of how **you** feel before a call or a presentation or a site visit.

My first face to face sales call years ago, after a week's sales training on Professional Selling Skills, saw me sit in the car for half an hour, petrified of meeting my first potential buyer. I was so nervous I would fail at the call and be unable to provide any value at all.

In my role as a mentor to sales professionals and leaders, I see exactly the same signs with my clients some thirty years later. They may not be physically sitting where I was, but many have the same thoughts as I did all those years ago. And the energy that shows up is a lack of certainty and conviction. The focus is usually on themselves instead of a clear, connected focus on their buyer and their buyer's future.

Sellers know how to build rapport, but what many don't know is how to truly connect.

The Birth of *The Connection Economy*

Peter Drucker stated that for a company to grow, it must do two things to succeed - innovate and market. I would like to add one more area of focus - they must connect! Marketer extraordinaire, Seth Godin, has coined our new economy, the *Connection Economy* for a reason.

We know that we can't build things any faster today nor can we make them any cheaper. In many instances, we can't make them any different so what will be the difference that make the difference?

In transitioning to another economy, we can't do business the old way and expect a different result. What matters today is sharing, trust, vulnerability, storytelling, leadership, humility and humanity. It's about realising the value is in our ROR – our return on relationships and not so much our ROI – our return on investment.

It's about people and it's about connecting.

- Connecting online
- Connecting with ourselves
- Connecting other people with other people

Technology is the one constant across the ages that has taken us into each new economy and it is allowing us to achieve different results today as well.

For thousands of years, civilisation survived in a hunter/gatherer environment until the invention of the wheel and the plough. This technology led us into the Agrarian economy where farming became the economic driver and then a more linear economy was created with the introduction of the printing press and the steam engine. Once again, this technology opened the world up and we headed into the Industrial Economy where farmers were enticed off the land and out of the Agrarian Economy with the security of regular pay packets, with employment in factories where the trade-off was to work long hours in thankless, boring assembly lines for the mass production of products to support their families. Institutions reigned supreme and were encouraged by the ideals of power and growth and the collection of profits. Arrogance, ignorance and complacency meant that businesses didn't believe they needed to change. It was working for them, they were being rewarded with their ivory towers and great profits, but they didn't anticipate the future and the fact that the world would eventually change.

Transitioning from the Industrial Economy to the Knowledge Economy began with the introduction of the computer and the internet and brought with it a new set of behaviours. Business intelligence allowed business to take information and use it strategically.

Communication opened up at all levels, sharing of information was more prevalent, ivory towers were being toppled, silos dismantled, open office plans adopted and reinvention occurring. Industries such as the railways and manufacturing plants were the first to notice those changes. The industries, companies and individuals who *got it* and innovated, marketed and connected, were the ones who sent a new message to the market - they read the writing on the wall and made the shift.

Xerox was one of those companies, not only shifting their commercial offering to the market, but also sharing the journey with their staff and sharing that knowledge using new tools that empowered us all to tell a new and compelling story.

As a sales executive at Xerox through those times in the 1990's, we were in the throes of moving from the analogue world to the digital world, encouraging our clients to buy and build repositories of data and knowledge to populate the technologies that housed them. My State Manager and National Knowledge Manager at the time, Andy Scott led us through that paradigm shift.

As a company, we were one of the first to study workplace knowledge by recognising the value of documents in knowledge sharing and sharing that information. What was discovered along this journey, was that 42% of knowledge was sitting in the brains of employees (tacit) and 58% was spread across paper documents, electronic documents and knowledge bases. (Source Delphi)

The question was, how much of this *tacit knowledge* was being shared and how could we encourage more of it to be shared with other employees? We all embraced these technological changes that information opened up for us, and we celebrated the fact we were leaders in the Knowledge Economy. Today, the business world is on the move again, and we find ourselves facing another paradigm shift in business with the ability to write another chapter in the history of commerce.

Today technology creates momentum again and has led us to *The Connection Economy*. Technology is still used for data and BI, but personal connection across technological platforms is accelerating. Today, through social engagement, our competitive advantage is gained through our relationships, our personal branding and those with whom we can leverage and connect and collaborate.

The Connection Economy is an environment that cares about purpose **and** profit. It is more connected to stakeholders than just the finances and shareholders. It is an environment that places value on people who are OK with transparency, vulnerability, contribution and who create meaningful art by owning what they are good at and sharing it.

Building a Bridge

Many people, sellers and leaders alike, have a deep-seated belief that money is *'hard to come by'*, they have been conditioned to believe *'money is the root of all evil'*, that sellers selling products are lining their own pockets first or that there is no room for nice people in business. They believe business must be a zero-sum game, with someone winning and someone losing. It is OK for this to happen between two competitors, of course, but not between a vendor and a client.

If you ask most businesses, or most sales leaders, what the purpose of business is, they will say it is to make a profit and that it's all about the numbers. And they will be partly right. This outlook, though, is the language of the Industrial Economy with a driving focus of control, profiteering and greed. An economy where there was little place for connection. A time that was so rules driven that people had to almost ask for permission to breathe, obey authority at the drop of a hat and when told to 'jump', ask 'how high?' An environment where masculine energy abounded, where sellers were intimidated in speaking with the CXO level, where they were afraid to challenge their buyer's thinking, where they were mindful of asking buyers for their money or how much they had in their budget, where they dared not say 'no', where they didn't create art to share and post for free in public places for the good of all, where they didn't care enough to care enough.

We can't afford to think that way today. It's time the meaning of connection was given more credence and focus than ever before. A combined top down and bottom up approach across an entire world is in order, where everyone - businesses, leaders and individuals all view themselves as *connectors* and not be defined by their roles, power or positions.

There are so many opportunities in any given day when we can connect, where we can build a bridge for someone, where we can add value and take a relationship to another level, whether it is upwards or sideways. Where we can make eye contact, smile, say thank you or connect one person to another. Our roles do not define who we are, yet many people rely only on their role to define them, and never truly connect with others because of the mask they believe they must wear to fit the role.

Seth Godin in his book, The Icarus Deception, shares how this *Connection Economy* has changed everything. The way we listen to music, the way we shop, the way we eat, the way we buy, the way we find romantic partners and the way we show up in the world of those around us. It has given us so much more choice and in doing so, put such a warranted emphasis on trust.

The Strongest Force in the Human Personality

The **law of commitment and consistency,** according to author Robert Cialdini in his book *'Influence: The Psychology of Persuasion'*, is the strongest force in the human personality because it allows us to remain consistent with how we see ourselves. We may put on masks to the world, but if we don't see ourselves as that person at an internal level then we will never be that person we paint ourselves to be at an external level. If you want to be the new breed of seller or sales leader and have the ability to connect with another human being at a level that **moves them,** then you need to trust them, and they need to trust you. If you want to be the new breed of seller, then you need to own your value, learn to share your work proudly and have an intention to make a difference in the world, or at least your buyer's world.

Taking responsibility, taking on board feedback, understanding our past conditioning and beliefs, being curious and wanting to listen to what is being said and not said, are examples of growth strategies that serve everyone. To truly connect with another, means to be present to them, and to you. To connect even more is to go past chitchat and instant rapport, and understand what really makes our buyer tick, at a deeper and broader level.

The Competitive Advantage

Technology has clearly given us a level of connection on an unprecedented global scale. We are connected to just about anything and anyone, at anytime and on any platform. We can find old school friends and rekindle relationships. We can become voyeurs and *date* people and still stay anonymous. We can have global conferences without getting out of our gym gear. Most of all we can run our business through this marvellous technology and connect with potential buyers at no cost by being keyboard warriors. With more and more people working from home and being more mobile, connection is a competitive advantage.

However, this *Connection Economy* can also ruin a business at the click of a mouse with an unhappy customer keying in honest feedback. After all, isn't perception still reality? This economy also changes the sales process. People don't go to you directly anymore, they connect with their social networks and their friends, they check out reviews online and they will source you when they're ready and not the other way around. *The Connection Economy* has made it so much easier for us with Forbes telling us that 78% of business transactions occur this way.

Connection with your buyers is more important than the features, advantages and benefits of your product or service. I think it's time to put away the conversations around feeds and speeds, strategy and tactics, bits and bytes and it's time to create meaning within our commercial conversations instead. To frame your outcomes in a way that connects the difference you will make for their world, in a way that contributes to their bottom line, as well as yours.

Shift the Conversation

To shift the conversation is to change your game. To step out of that world of compliance where doing something because it's always been done that way is the norm. It's time to not just break the rules but create some new rules. Tell some new stories. Risk failure. Put yourself out there and ask the odd question you wouldn't have asked in the past. In doing so you will shift your status quo.

To grow you, your team, your business or your client's business cannot be done by staying the same and playing safe. It's about doing work that has meaning and importance. This is *The Connection Economy*. It's about *the art of commercial conversations* and joining all the different dots.

You just have to look at the icons of our time and check out the following messages, their manifestos and their meaning on business as they articulate shifting **their** conversations.

From Steve Jobs – *"Apple should strive for an intimate connection with customers' feelings"*. And they do.

From Richard Branson – In his first meetings with Japanese businessmen in the early 80s, Branson was amazed at the politeness and the respect they gave young Branson despite his shaggy-sweater jean-wearing appearance. The Japanese taught Richard to *always treat everyone in your business with respect, not just those that you need to impress. Someday you could be doing business with them.* And he did.

From Oprah Winfrey – *'The ability to connect, listen, and grow with others is essential in our professional growth. Relationships are always changing—and typically if they're not growing, they're dying. We must be intentional about our business relationships, giving them the time and attention that are necessary to nurture them.'* And she does.

So, it's time to make things mean more than your market and more than your role. It's time to consider how you position you, how you convey your intention and how it links to the reality of those around you. In this chain there are four key links:

The Connection Chain

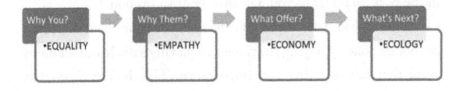

- People need to know who you are, what you do and where you've come from. They need to know *'why you'* to feel trust so nobody feels more inferior or superior to the other. (Equality)
- You need to know about the people you want to meet, understand their worlds so they know you care about both them and their worlds. (Empathy)
- You need to know what you are offering them and why that should matter to them, and they must be able to articulate how leveraging your value will grow their business. (Economy)

- You both need to know about the important role you play in each other's worlds, what it means and what it will lead to, not just for today but the future. (Ecology)

Connecting is more than just making contact and building rapport.

Remove the Monkey Mind

At Dreamforce 2014, Arianna Huffington sat cross legged on a stage (her version of a childhood dream of sitting on a cloud) with a room full of business leaders, both men and women. Sitting upright, their eyes closed, hands open, palms upwards, breathing deeply they were connecting at a deeper level with themselves, in order to create a greater impact in their connection with others. In doing so knowing this would impact their business results as well.

We spend more time connecting our iPads, iPhones and iPods than we do connecting with ourselves – our iDentity, yet this is where the long term, sustainable change will happen.

When we have connected with who we are, when we are centred and grounded and respect the value we bring and the purpose of our actions, things begin to flow. Mindfulness is a key component in connecting with another and has proven benefits to business. All it takes is anywhere from 30 seconds to 30 minutes to experience a real, tangible shift.

When we focus our mind on something we can see, hear or feel and allow ourselves to still the busy chatter of the mind, we are totally present to any conversation. We don't have to stress about what we're going to say in our meeting, or what we should have done at the last meeting, or how much overwhelm and confusion we are feeling. Instead, it helps promote more clarity in our thinking.

The 2,500-year-old Buddhist practice of mindfulness helps us remove the *'monkey mind'*, a Buddhist term for confusion, overwhelm, indecision, anxiety and a host of emotional states we find ourselves in today.

Imagine connecting with a client where your energy levels were manic, rushed and muddled. Imagine connecting with a client where you are on purpose, calm and have real clarity around the outcome. Where sensing this in you, by default, they also sense you have their best interests at heart. What level of control, respect and authority do you usually portray?

27 Minutes a Day

27 minutes a day, according to Harvard neuroscientists, will change our brain structure and brain patterns over a short eight-week period. The home of our 'fight, flight and freeze zone' is the primitive part of the brain called the amygdala. This physically shrinks after relaxation and attention (aka mediation and mindfulness). This means we are able to process stressful situations a lot more effectively and experience more clarity and reason.

The change shows up as a really proven and biological increase in our well being and quality of life and we are able to balance out that looping tape recording that keeps playing those same worries, plans, stresses, must do's and can't do's that plague many of us from the moment we wake up to the moment we fall asleep.

So powerful is this concept that businesses are now recommending mindfulness to sellers and executives, as well as stressed employees, to strengthen connection with others. Schools are having teachers trained in mindfulness, so children can begin to have quiet time on the mat again – memories many of us might remember ourselves.

Today, we have to do more with less, manage budgets that are constantly increasing, fight time deadlines and operate with minimal resources, so having such a natural and cost-effective way to be more productive and generate growth in revenue and relationships is a real leveller. No different to the introduction and priority of exercise and clean eating improving the quality of our personal lives.

Listening is Not Enough

Why I encourage sellers to spend a few minutes prior to a call grounding themselves is because it helps them own their calls. Too many sellers let their emotions get the better of them on a customer visit because they are not prepared, they wing the call and they have no idea what to say and when. Too many of them are also uncomfortable with silence – a major component of mindfulness. As a result, they feel they have to fill the gaps when, if they simply realised silence is golden so that people can process information, they would be less likely to jump in or lose the thread by thinking ahead about what to say next.

What would make a huge difference is if they learned to leave their emotions at the door and be totally present to every conversation. But listening is not enough, they need to actually hear what is being said – the story behind the story or the problem behind the problem, as well as what is **not** being said. When we can control our breathing, it helps us be comfortable with silence and when we can do both, we are so much more powerful and give ourselves such a competitive advantage.

Leave Your Emotions at The Door

The ability to practice mindfulness prior to business meetings is critical. Considering most CXO/decision makers want to get straight to the point, give nothing away and expect you to work for your time, many sellers get rattled and resort to their emotions. And by emotions I don't mean they need to reach for the box of tissues. What I mean by resorting to emotions is when someone is in their head and listens to the voices of the internal critic at the expense of the buyer's words. Where they don't ask quality questions and skip important parts of the conversation, ultimately losing control of the entire conversation.

Where the seller leaves on a high, goes straight back to the office and high fives that they've got an awesome new prospect. Why? Because they believe the buyer likes them. By not being present and in control, their emotions lead them just like the elephant in the jungle. As a result, they will either lose the opportunity to the competition, will be fed excuses or the buyer does nothing, and they wonder what went wrong with this *great* relationship they had.

These sellers could have the best sales skills in the world, but their mindset and lack of emotional discipline will spoil any potential opportunity. Learning to practice mindfulness in connecting with people is crucial today.

Let's Play....

To boost your connection with yourself and others, it's about knowing how to become mindful. So how do you do that on the job and what's it really all about? Mindfulness to me is like putting everything that is swirling around my head onto a metaphorical shelf for a while and focussing on one thing. I'm mindful 'the shelf' is there and I don't ignore what's sitting on it. However, I hold it long enough to gain some perspective on what's important, using my breath to create a calm state.

It is effectively a short-term state change through breathing, which contributes to a long-term trait change in who you are and what you bring to the table.

Just as change is one of life's constants, so is breathing. We can use our breathing to do more than just keep us alive. We can use it to help us be *'in the moment,'* and be present because when we leverage it effectively, our brain undergoes structural changes that help us relax and lose those unresourceful emotional constraints.

The simplicity of breathing in through the nose and out through the nose triggers a relaxing response in us. Try it now. Breathe in through the nose and out through the nose and keep your mouth closed. Do this ten-times! It will slow your breathing down and allow you to be totally present to the moment giving you the ability to focus even more. When you breathe through your mouth, not only do you take in unfiltered toxins, but it triggers an anxious response, your heart rate increases, and your thinking stays cloudy or scattered.

For those of us who need a quick fix of confidence prior to a meeting or adrenalin pumping moment, all we need is thirty seconds. Just like Arianna Huffington took hundreds of executives on a one-minute journey, we have the ability to take ourselves on the same journey at the drop of a hat.

Gratitude is the Antidote

From a sales perspective, who you connect with matters and who you are, matters even more. At the end of the day it's about you, being you, being open to growth and being grateful for your strengths and value. As Oscar Wilde so fittingly said, *"Be yourself because everyone else is already taken."* And in the context of being comfortable with yourself and the value you bring, I think it can be summed up by the late and great Maya Angelou who commented, *"I don't trust people who don't love themselves and then tell me, 'I love you'."*

You are 37% more effective as a seller, according to the Harvard Business Review, when you keep a record of what you are grateful for because it keeps you purposeful, resilient and connected.

When people like who you are and what you stand for, when they think you are like them and they feel connected and trust you, then they will be even more responsive toward you. That's what we want from our buyers and that's the biggest thing they want from us.

So, to know your buyers, and for them to feel they know you, it's important to lose the need for approval and perfectionism. It's about being open to feedback and even the possibility of failure, as that is where the learning lies and a key component of success.

The quickest way to do that is to stare down the person in the mirror. You have no need to feel desperate, or not enough, or needy or subservient to your buyer. You don't have to walk on eggshells around people when you know your value. It's realising there is no hierarchy and no invisible pedestal that your buyer, or anyone else for that matter, is standing on.

We are all equal. Others will be an expert in their field and you will be an expert in your field. Between the two of you, imagine the business dealings you can have when you realise you are both the same, but different.

Stand in your conviction, break a few rules, connect with what is important and you will be more than ready to make that first contact with your buyer. The next chapter will lead you there... turn the page and join us. But first, complete the following self-assessment:

SELF REFLECTION

- What is the one internal resource you draw on to show up, be present and connect more effectively in the moment with the buyer?

....

....

- Why is that important?

....

....

- Did you feel yourself feeling more grounded with the mindfulness exercise?

  Yes or No

'People can't be just tied together. They have to connect. Otherwise they'll find themselves bound hand and foot.'

Ai Yazawa

CONTACT

THE ART OF SOCIAL

It's about BEING social, not just being ON social. It's more than a playground where we go to play, it's like being in an auditorium where we can team up, play our hearts out and be seen by those who will see our value.

MAKING CONTACT IS more than reaching out and touching someone's hand, as so deftly sung by Diana Ross. It's also more than having a sender, a receiver and a message in between. It's realising with all the noise and feedback and frequencies at play today, that we need to get very clear on what makes people tick and understand how we can create cut-through when we do contact people.

We Are Social Creatures

Let's step back in time for a minute and let's revisit the evolution of social interaction. Let's understand what matters to human beings from a communication perspective.

From the dawn of time, cave drawings, smoke signals and storytelling were all ways to make contact and spread our message. We eventually evolved our platforms with the printing press, paper and believe it or not, pigeons. All were vehicles used to contact another person. These were followed by the telegraph, telegrams and telephony, ultimately allowing the world to open up even more. These platforms have continued to evolve, and we now have all things internet – the most technologically social platform of all!

Yet, how social are we, as humans? How many of us are keyboard warriors, afraid to meet people, afraid to pick up the phone or afraid to really get to know someone? How successful are we, as sellers, in differentiating ourselves and getting our foot into new doors, or even existing doors, for that matter?

As a human species we are wired to be social. Couples, clans or wider communities, we all seek connectedness through people who are like us, and who we like and trust.

We also socialise with different people in different seasons of our life. As teenagers we hang out with other teenagers. As parents we socialise with other parents, and as business people we relate to other business people who share our interests, values and belief systems.

Technology has allowed us to search for old friends, evaluate new friends and contact just about anyone, all the while enabling people to also contact us. All at the press of a button or the click of a mouse.

As a community, our ability to share so much more of ourselves has been amplified through social channels. We are able to network, share stories, distribute case studies, reveal photos, showcase new product launches, provide social status updates, amplify personal marketing, create information portals and even enrol in online dating. Social platforms are not a fad or a phase. We are in the *Connection Economy* and these platforms are, in effect, today's modern-day cave walls.

Push Versus Pull

In the old world, to contact a potential buyer was very much a push mentality. We had few other options. It was our responsibility to instigate and drive contact with our potential buyers, because if we didn't, they would never know we existed. And when we did eventually meet with them, it was so simple and uncomplicated, because many were ignorant when it came to what was available to them in the wider world. They had no way to research us, or our products. They trusted us. In many cases, that trust was abused with sellers who *'stitched them up'* or *'did a deal'*.

What was important in the past was what was said long after we walked **out** of the room.

What's important today is what is said long before we even walk **into** the room.

We've been given tools that can ruin us, as much as glorify us. They can disengage us as quickly as engage us. They can make us less social, or more social – it depends how we choose to leverage these tools.

The one key thing to remember is that we must still actively pursue opportunities and relationships. Whilst we still risk potential rejection, just as we did prior to these tools coming along, we still must engage personally. That means being aware of both our personal brand and our professional message to the market.

Making Contact Just Got More Interesting

Television took thirteen years to reach fifty million viewers, internet service providers took three years to sign their Fifty millionth subscriber, Facebook just a year to hit fifty million users, Twitter took nine months and Angry Birds? Thirty-five days!! We are contacting new connections at a speed that is unprecedented. If our intention is to contribute to others, then the scale and opportunity for our message to be received by our market is enormous, if we leverage it smartly. And that means online as well as offline, and inbound as well as outbound.

Some say it is because of social that **cold calling** is dead. According to the Harvard Business Review, 90% of decision makers say they never respond to cold calls today. 72% of Americans have signed up for the *do not call* register, yet the number one challenge from sellers is, *'How do I get an appointment via the phone?'*

Some say **direct mail** is dead. An Epsilon study found that 67% of consumers found direct mail offers are more trustworthy than *online* offers. Especially when personal, targeted and followed up. Word on the street is more people are reverting to strategic mail deliveries that get opened, and also provide more meaning and value.

Some say **email** is dead. According to McKinsey's iConsumer survey, there was a twenty percent decline in e-mail usage from 2008, yet Forester confirms that the volume of emails is increasing. With more and more people being time poor and complaining of email overload, does this mean more and more emails are being sent and received but are not being read? *'How do I create cut through?'* is the most common question salespeople ask.

What about **voicemail**? Some businesses are stopping all voicemail channels completely – Coca Cola being one. They have given their employees the opportunity to turn off their voicemail with only 6% opting to keep it. Their reality is that checking voicemails constantly disrupts productivity, and if important enough, people will call, email or text instead. With research showing that only 30% of workers listen to voicemails, the number one question I am asked is, *'What do I say to get people to return my call?'* Maybe, the answer is as simple as nothing!!

Statistics are telling us that our buyers are hanging out on **social** more and more. 85% of B2B buyers believe companies should present their information via social networks (Iconsive).

It therefore makes sense that those businesses, and sellers, who have a great credible profile, a strong professional message and an engaging personal formula for making contact, will be more attractive to the potential buyer. This becomes a pull approach.

If we consider that 81% of B2B purchase cycles start with an online search, and 90% of buyers say when they are ready to buy, *'they'll find you'* (Earnest Agency), you best make sure you can be found.

For me personally, and because *I want people to find me*, LinkedIn is my chosen platform to make contact and socialise with my potential prospects. It is the lane where my target market plays (B2B sellers, sales leaders, business owners and CXOs). It has helped me create a strong brand in the sales leadership space, and as a result, I have experienced tangible results by way of invitations to speak overseas, to train sales teams, coach and mentor sales leaders, and be invited into think tanks.

Receiving an unsolicited call from a potential buyer is something every seller wants to experience, but very rarely does. We all want our value to be perceived highly enough so we become an attraction magnet to any potential opportunity. There is a difference though between waiting reactively for someone to contact you and proactively approaching opportunities in a professional and value driven way, using all platforms. And to do that well means we all need to understand our market, our message and our medium.

To be a player in the future is seeing that the future is now. How do you become a player?

Engaging Our Buyers

According to the late Chet Holmes in his book, 'The Ultimate Sales Machine', only three percent of any audience are in the market to buy right now. If you were to ask any audience 'who would be interested in buying in the next six months?', seven percent would more than likely raise their hands, thirty percent wouldn't be thinking about it at all, thirty percent would show no interest and thirty percent would *never* be interested.

The broad-brush picture looks like this: If we consider that only three percent of the buying public, across any genre, are ready to buy anything, right now, today, then shouldn't that change how we go to market and how we contact our potential buyers?

If that means only three percent are ready for a commercial conversation right now, then why do so many sellers' conversations revolve around buyers buying *today*? Shouldn't our commercial conversations be respectful enough to know where our buyers sit within these percentages? Wouldn't it make more sense to lose the attachment to doing a deal in those cases, rather than risk closing non-closable buyers and potentially losing the opportunity all together?

Surely, it's a no brainer that we nurture the remaining ninety percent of those relationships by creating a combination of value *and* disruption. Enough so that we position ourselves front of mind for when they *do* decide to invest in change. Imagine if we did that rather than putting so much energy and emphasis on closing deals just for today? And if we did, would the buyer be more receptive to engaging with us earlier, and for longer?

With buyers not wanting to answer our calls, return our messages or find the time to meet for twenty minutes, we need to do something different. According to Forester, 14% of people who sell admitted they don't know how to differentiate themselves from their competition. The reason is that they don't have clarity around their message. They aren't able to have these commercial conversations that enable them to even meet the key person, let alone have the opportunity to disrupt that person's status quo.

More than anything, it's important to realise there are no shortcuts. When you combine a spirit of contribution, a great qualification process, an intention of growth and a message oozing with commercial value, then you bring so much relevance and attractiveness to the table. You become more of a designer, a producer of sorts. In fact, you become an artist.

In the words of Seth Godin,

"Art isn't only a painting. Art is anything that's creative, passionate, and personal. And great art resonates with the viewer, not only with the creator. An artist is someone who uses bravery, insight, creativity, and boldness to challenge the status quo. And an artist takes it personally. Art is a personal gift that changes the recipient. The medium doesn't matter. The intent does."

As artists, salespeople and sales leaders need to take the responsibility of their role personally. They need clarity around their intent and the confidence and conviction to articulate it.

Articulating Our Message

We are fortunate today, in that we have something our predecessors didn't have. We have this amazing opportunity to showcase ourselves as experts in our field, to connect with anyone we want and to build our own personal brand. However, to do it succinctly, we need a framework to help us language it across different situations. Networking environments, appointment calling, segueing within conversations and positioning ourselves in our proposals and presentations.

What this means is that the value of our message must resonate more with the buyer than us, the seller.

I was challenged to create a Messaging Matrix for salespeople after first being inspired by my mentor, at the time, Thought Leaders Global founder, Matt Church's positioning statement. I believe that we don't need an elevator pitch that remains static and uncomfortable. What we do need is a framework where we can play tic tac toe, create soundbites for our back pocket or act out vignettes that can be called on at any given time, depending on who we are with, to help us create alignment, bridge gaps or fill holes in any conversation.

When people connect with a strong message, they are moved, and they act.

So, let's unpack this Messaging Matrix framework to see how we do this in the true spirit of social so that we can get seen, get known and get business.

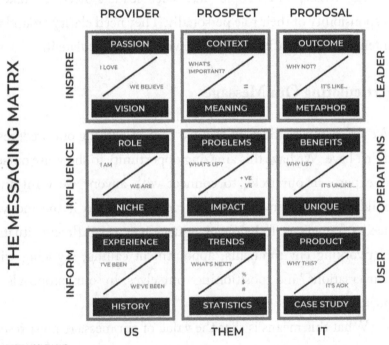

© BERNADETTE MCCLELLAND

You will notice this model has two axes. Vertically, there is reference to us and our company as providers. Next is all about the prospect and why them? This is followed by us introducing our proposed solution and partnership. It's how we position ourselves, how we think and how we sell.

There is another pattern that you can probably see, and this relates to the approach based on the hierarchical level within your customer base. The three levels are

- informational approach usually suited to the 'user' level because they are interested in the details, proof, specifications and the product
- the influential approach is usually suited to an operational level because they are more into the day to day running of the business and are looking for ways to improve efficiencies and productivity
- the inspirational approach is usually designed for leadership, or the decision maker level, where they are more strategic, big picture and not into the details as much as the lower levels.

When we overlay both patterns on each other we have nine different soundbites, and nine different vignettes. We can access these at any time, allowing us to be more spontaneous and present at the same time. It removes the awkwardness of following some scripted elevator pitch and allows us to dance within an elegant and relevant framework.

This is an example of what I might say if I was using **all** the soundbites and vignettes from the matrix.

'To keep it simple, I'm a keynote speaker as well as a sales performance trainer/coach. As CEO of 3 Red Folders, we work with sales teams typically in the manufacturing, construction, ICT and Aged Care space. This allows me to pivot off my background as a sales executive role in Fortune 500 companies prior to owning my own wholesale business and moving into a leadership role.

What lights me up in my role today, is working with sales teams where everyone get those great moments of clarity, where they intuitively go 'ahhh...I get it!' Why does that matter so much to me? Because I believe salespeople are the heroes and heroines of the business world and them 'getting it' is key to their growth and the business growth.

There are three key problems I see my clients face though: staff retention, not making their numbers and not being able to differentiate themselves, and the impact can be huge. Profits and performance take a nose dive and stress increases. Statistics are already telling us that less than 50% of companies are actually making their numbers, and the trend moving forward is showing that skill-sets will definitely need to shift from that traditional hard core focus.

What it's really all about is positioning ourselves exclusively, thinking laterally and selling consciously. This means businesses have to start thinking outside the square when it comes to what's involved with their business growth.

At 3 Red Folders, we provide bespoke solutions for our clients based on an evaluation and needs analysis where we dig in around strategy, messaging, questioning and qualification - and why it is not happening - so our clients can start to see their pipeline flow rather than being bloated. Our most recent client has already seen a revenue growth of between 50 and 60% within six months and it's because we operate at that intersection of sales process, psychology and science – it's something very unique. We're kind of like 'the sales profession's first responders'.

Does this mean you need to use every point on the matrix? No.

But it does help if you can have them in your back pocket ready to roll off your tongue at any given moment. To be so 'in tune' with your flow, to be so 'present' to a conversation, to be so confident in leading a dialogue.

So, let's dig deeper and peel back the layers of this framework so you can create your own.

The Provider - This is About You and Your Company

Expertise / History

[I've Been] - What has been your experience? Where have you come from? 10 years ago, 5 years ago, last year? Keep it short and simple.

[We've Been] - What about your company's history. What is the brand story, what got them into business? What was that short, sharp journey they have been on. People love stories.

Role/Niche

[I Am...] - This is simply what you do. Don't try to overcomplicate the role to sound like everybody else. You do what you do. Speak in language people understand. 'I am a sales consultant or 'I am a keynote speaker'.

[We Are...] - The same applies to your company. What is the niche you operate in? Who is your target market? What are you known for?

Passion/Vision

[I Love...] - What lights YOU up about your role? Is it seeing customers succeed, is it because you love being autonomous, is it because you are making a difference? Find it and language it.

[We Believe…] - What is something you take a stand on? What do you see making a difference in the future? People like to work with companies with a purpose, a vision and an opinion.

The Prospect - This is About Them and Their Company

Trends/Statistics

[What's Next?] Trends are something that is always a conversation starter, but it must be about **their** environment and **their** industry – not yours. Identifying key changes will always allow you to expand and move into potential challenges as a result of these trends.

[%, $ #] – Statistics provide evidence. Evidence gives people the why behind something. Statistics give credibility to a theory. You can do this by citing metrics that include dollars, percentages, time, numbers or energy. Besides, don't they say 37% of statistics are made up on the spot?

Challenges/Impact

[What's Up?] Every business has challenges and when you can come to the table with an understanding of what they are, you demonstrate that 'you get them'. This, in turn, breeds trust. The brain works in threes so collate a few typical challenges and ask for their thoughts.

[-ve and +ve] People are driven by avoidance or achievement. Your solution will do both by either providing a positive impact to their business or by helping them avoid a negative impact from occurring. Your responsibility is to help the buyer identify one, or both. For example, 'As a salesperson, what is the negative impact if you continued to miss your target?' or as a business owner, 'What is the

positive impact of your sales team increasing their key performance activities?' You don't tell them. They tell you.

Context/Meaning

[=] We are meaning makers which means we all put our own interpretation on events or words. It's important we understand the angle our buyer is coming from within a conversation and not just assume. This is why it's important to ask something so simple as, "... what does that mean to you?" It's why checking in is so important.

[What's It About?] – When we can isolate what something is really all about, it creates agreement. After all, business is about agreement. When we can agree on a higher purpose, for example, *business growth* as opposed to *sales training*, it opens the conversation up for broader discussion. Too many salespeople hang around in the detail and content of their product, therefore, losing their relevance.

The Proposal - This is About Your Product and Partnership

Case Study/Product

[It's AOK] - This taps into social proof. People love to be able to relate to someone who is like them and to hear their journey to success. Have a case study in your back pocket that relates to your buyer, that has an outcome and also has a metric, whether that be percentage, dollars, or time.

[Why This?] - Identifying what you sell and why is key. Product knowledge from a features, advantages and benefits perspective

gives you the foundation to reverse Engineer your benefits back into questions. It allows you to not tell, but ask, so the prospect begins to tell you the benefits of your solution instead.

Benefits/Uniqueness

[Why Us?] Value is what your buyer wants, but not around just your product. It's about your ideas as well. A value model is contextual and helps them see where they want to go (status). It also demonstrates what is going to get them there (stages) as well as a currency of sorts or ROI. Your role is to be able to demonstrate your value by meeting all three.

[It's Unlike…] - Whereas a metaphor is *like something*, you also need to find what you are *unlike*. What makes you different when you are in the sea of sameness? Apart from you being the differentiator, stand for something, because if your competition can say the same as you, then you have nothing unique to offer. There will be something about a process, or who you work with, or what you offer outside of your product, that is specific to you. For example, what makes **our** sales performance practice unique is that we operate at the intersection of sales process, psychology and science – and nobody else says that.

Outcome/ Metaphor

[It's Like…] - If a picture paints a thousand words, then a metaphor paints a brilliant picture. Sometimes we need to step away from logic and shift our buyer to imagination. A metaphor is when something is *like something*. It's a shortcut which means you don't need to explain a thing. It's kind of like *joining the dots* for them.

[Why Not?] – How strong is your conviction? You have gained agreement, got granular and gone big picture. You've addressed all personality styles and touched them at a head level, a hand level and a heart level. What is the next logical step you want to take? Take it! Ask it!

You need to remember that there are three questions your buyers will be asking themselves at a subconscious level, about you, when you make contact. Those questions will be, *'What are you known for knowing?'*, *'What do you know about my industry, my business, my role?'* and, *'What is the value you bring to me as a person?'*

When you work your squares well, and you work them into conversations, appointment making calls, segues when moving from rapport to business and even in your proposals, presentations and bios, you will see how much more effective you will be. You will hear the lightness in your approach, feel yourself relax and your confidence increase. Most of all, you will notice how you position yourself as an expert in your field.

Turn the page and learn how to pivot off your message and strengthen those social skills to deepen your contact with your buyer even more. Become a relevant storyteller.

To wrap this chapter up, consider the following:

SELF REFLECTION

What is the major value you provide when contacting your buyers and your clients through *the art of social*? Is your aim to:

- expand your database?
- demonstrate your role as a thought leader?

- allow others to connect with you?
- create a personal one on one connection?
- create a community you can provide value to?

1. Which is the channel you prefer to use, and do you have a strategy for making contact? If so, what is it?

....
....
....

2. Articulate your message using all the squares.

....
....
....

3. Where do you feel your credibility, branding and realness sit on a scale of 0 to 10 and what can you do to move the needle?

....
....
....

Social media allows me to pick my times for social interaction.

Guy Kawasaki

BOOK TWO

THINK!

THE VALUE OF YOUR OFFERING AND YOUR THOUGHT LEADERSHIP

CONTENT

THE ART OF STORY

*It's more than features, advantages and benefits. It's the
ability to tell a story that captivates and spread that story
to the world through messages that create value.*

LANDING IN A new country with only $200 and a suitcase,
led me to answering an ad in the local newspaper.

**'WANTED: Door to Door Sellers. Stationery Sets for
Multiple Sclerosis. Commission Only. Immediate Start'**

I decided to *give it a go* and so began my first foray into the world
of selling. In a foreign land and a climate that was a shock to my
system, it was obvious my body would have been better suited to the
slopes of Switzerland than the tropical heat of Queensland. All that
aside, I began pounding the pavements of Mt Gravatt in Brisbane,

shaking the bushes to make enough money to take me the rest of the way around Australia - this eighteen-year old's holiday of a lifetime.

House after house and door after door, everybody would open their wallets – and their homes. Some would invite me in for a cool drink of water, glass of lemonade or refreshing juice. On one occasion, even lunch. I remember it well! What was it that made them do that? Apart from the sweat pouring off me and probably feeling sorry for this young, fair-skinned, freckled-faced kid, I was certain it was the stories I was telling them. Stories that would connect them with the real message and the brave recipients behind the purchase of these stationery sets. It was connecting the difference their few dollars would make to the lives of these kids with MS. But more than the dollars, it was being made aware of the difference they personally would make.

And whilst, facts are what we use to tell, stories are what we use to sell. And stories help us sell any difference!

Stories are Ideas Dressed Up

One Friday evening over a year ago, my mobile phone rang. Curious as to who was calling me after 8pm, I was surprised to find it was a contact I had made from a cold call about eighteen months earlier (proof that prospecting must never stop). He was now in charge of a national sales team at a new company. Whilst apologising for calling me at such a late hour and at such short notice, he asked if he could book me the following week to speak at his sales kickoff conference. As part of our negotiation discussions a few days later, his Managing Director walked into our meeting, sat down and asked me what I knew about his company. I told him the story of how NASA had used their product in space. He smiled and walked out.

1. As a seller I knew my prospect's story and appreciated his emotional pride and connection with that story.
2. As a prospect, he appreciated me knowing his story and acknowledging its worth.

What is the story behind your business or your product?

If you were to 'test' someone on what they knew about your business, what story would you want them to deliver? Every story we deliver must have real meaning regardless of whether it is a model drawn on a napkin over coffee, a proposal given in a bound document or a presentation on a projector in a boardroom.

We want to hear these stories because they mean so much more than the statistics, spreadsheets and strategies that drive business. When we hear a story that resonates, we buy into that story, we become part of that story. In business, having someone buy into a story we are telling, can be such a competitive advantage and prove priceless.

To embed this theory, a colleague of mine in his new appointment as global president for a security software company, scheduled impromptu field visits with his sellers. As they left the car, he would ask them to leave all collateral behind. This meant that they couldn't rely on content that revolved around product. It meant they couldn't lean on the brochure but had to converse instead, and it meant asking quality questions and weaving in relevant stories. Did it push them into a state of panic? Many of them, yes! Surprisingly, it was the senior sellers. Did they elicit customer concerns and understand what was really important? Absolutely!

The Power of a Story

Do you remember the real message the Tortoise and the Hare gave us? Or the magic meaning behind the Emperor's New Clothes? Or the simple complexity behind the randomness of Dr Seuss?

How many of us would like to see ourselves as the hero in our favourite movie? How often do we connect with our past through the words of a song, or read an article that has us nodding in agreement?

The reality is that stories, whether they are shared before bed or before the Board, are so powerful when it comes to the scale and depth of our communication, to our breadth of learning and our retention of a message.

When we are told stories as a child we feel safe and close to the person reading us the story - safe enough to fall asleep.

As we grow up, we read stories of super heroes and princesses and we pretend to be like them. We dress like them, we act out scenes from their stories, we hold hairbrushes in front of mirrors. In our minds, we become them. Physically, mentally and emotionally we place ourselves front and centre into the story as we step into their character.

As we get older, we hear stories from others and we consciously and subconsciously relate those stories to our own experiences, especially when there has been a connection to a challenge faced, a pain experienced or a dark spot where we failed.

As a potential buyer, I would much rather hear a story that means something to me. A story that might fill a void or show me the light at the end of the tunnel (without me having to admit my world might actually exist within a tunnel and without a light). In essence, a story that resonates with me, is relevant and takes me to a place that is better than my status quo.

The shift needed for sellers in this new era of selling is to embrace strong storytelling skills, because the story can no longer just be about the features, advantages and benefits of what we sell.

The Biased Lens or the Buyers Lens

There are two stories that are important to tell. One story is your story and the other story is your buyer's story.

Your story will always be about the benefit and value you offer to others through **your** eyes.

Your buyer's story will always be their perception of your value to them through **their** eyes. Most sellers only tell the first story.

To share with one business owner the journey of another business owner, or one leader the journey of another, and share the respective challenges and wins they each experienced is powerful. What is critical, therefore, is for you to know **how** to tell these stories with meaning and impact.

One way to deliver a story around value to a prospective buyer is to ask an existing buyer one simple question, *'What is the business difference we have made to your business?'*

It is so easy for us to espouse the value of what we are selling because we view it through our biased lens. We must understand the value received through the buyer's lens, and that can only be achieved by asking them. Once we have our buyer's answer to that solitary question, we are able to articulate the benefits we offer with more conviction. This helps us create a case study or a success story to share that is received with more credibility. By default, we unleash our own value even more.

What is Your Story?

My most favourite task when working with sellers is to understand what **they** believe to be their story. Initially, it surrounds them. It surrounds the length of time they have been in business, the history of the business, the product range of the business, their pricing structure, how they offer the best service and what **they** believe the value to be based on **their** experiences, wishes and dreams. This is **your** perception of value. To sell consciously is to understand your **buyer's** reason for buying.

I once worked with a sales team who sold office supplies and whose target market was the education sector. I asked the group what their buyer was looking for when their buyer went to market. The answers were varied. They ranged from the buyer wanting '*excellent service*' and '*lowest price*' to the buyer expecting '*quality products*.' When we asked the buyer the same question (in this case the school's Business Manager), her answer was vastly different. She said, we want '*more enrolments*' and '*value for prospective students*.'

How opposite were both these stories on the spectrum of seller/buyer alignment?

Cavemen with Briefcases

Every story has a hero. Our role is to firstly, define the hero. And it is not the seller!

Our second role is to identify where they are in their story and that begins with strong, curiosity-based questions.

Imagine asking a simple question, such as - *'What triggered your initial decision to go to market?'*

When a seller asks these extra questions and listens for the real story behind the story, pennies drop. *'Wow, we didn't know that is what goes on in a buyer's mind or within their process before they decide to buy. It actually has nothing to do with us'*, or, *'We didn't know that was the real difference we made'*. Value is in the eye of the beholder, namely the buyer.

Being able to share in these impact statements creates the basis for us to offer so much more of a compelling message than giving a buyer the features, advantages and benefits of our solutions.

And that is why Alan Kay's passage here is so apt, *"Scratch the surface in a typical boardroom and we're all just cavemen with briefcases, hungry for a wise person to tell us stories."*

Reflect on that quote for a moment. 'we're all just cavemen with briefcases.' We may not be running around wearing loin cloths and hunting the woolly mammoth, but evolution aside, we still have the same basic needs as our Neanderthal predecessors - give me a story so that I can recognise something that will help me do what I am supposed to do and be who I need to be.

Metaphors are Heart-tools that help us explore new ideas by bypassing the rational brain. A bit like a shortcut for the brain. They help us see how something is like something else. They help us connect something that is 'less understood' with something that is 'more understood'. They help our buyers understand something they previously may not have understood – a bit like us helping them join the dots – and of course, that was another metaphor!

Reimagining Your Happy Ending

According to Forrester, only 20% of salespeople have stories to tell and 78% of buyers believe sellers do not have enough relevant case studies, metaphors, analogies or stories to make a difference.

Let's just ponder that a moment.

Reflect on your proposals, or the PowerPoint presentations or even the story you tell when trying to make an appointment with a prospect. Take a look at the first 25% of either your proposal and/or your presentation or record yourself on that prospecting call. What information do you lead with? What story are you telling and who are you positioning as the hero? In most cases you will lead with your company information, your mission statement, your outcome or your product because it makes you feel safe and in control.

Try instead, to lead with the top three challenges your buyer, the hero in your story, typically faces. Lead with a mini-story, something akin to, *'In our experience the top three challenges business owners face are 1, 3 and 3. Which one do you find is most relevant to your environment?'*

Use this *Assumptive Ask* formula so your buyer understands that, *'you get them.'*

One of the biggest sales mantras we have had drummed into us as sellers was, 'we should never assume', but when we take an assumptive stance it's because we know our buyer's stories so well, we position ourselves as experts. And when we do that well, we allow them to buy into their own story.

- Are you able to articulate three of your buyer's challenges, right now?
- Are you able to articulate what the negative impact of these challenges are on your buyer and/or their business?

- Are you able to articulate three of your buyer's priorities, right now?
- Are you able to articulate what achieving these priorities means to your buyer and/or their business?

Perhaps these four points are something you might spend a few minutes contemplating before your next customer visit.

Create Leverage

In business, stories are also important because they help our buyers position themselves within particular scenarios. They provide an emotional gateway that helps them articulate and leverage that emotion to make change happen. We simply need to remember the age-old adage that 'people will always buy on emotion and back it up with logic'.

As the Greek mathematician Archimedes said, *"Give me a lever long enough and a place to put the fulcrum, and I will move the world."* It's about understanding what that lever is for your buyer, what is driving them and what resources they have for support.

To create leverage is to understand the gap. The gap from where they are to where they want to be. If they say things are going well, then what's the gap between going well and best practice? Ask them, don't guess. Asking questions, being curious will provide insights and help them identify that gap themselves. To help them think deeper, is to ask provocative questions. It is to effectively coach them through the process. It also means listening **through** their answers. It's listening for the stories behind their stories. What are they **not** saying?

Aristotle introduced us to a basic story structure of Act 1 (The Beginning), Act II (The Middle) and Act III (The End). When you ask well-constructed questions, buyers will tell you their stories with the same structure. They won't know it, but someone who is skilled at listening for the storyline, the problem behind the problem, will allow the space for each 'act' to be told. There is truth in the quote, 'silence is golden'. But how many sellers have the emotional discipline to stay silent enough to hear the story? The story may be as brief as only one sentence with a beginning, a middle and an end and yet we still find a way to interrupt! Give your buyers time to process your questions and they will reward you with their story!

The Problem Behind the Problem

I had not long been out of sales training as a sales trainee with Xerox and had been given all the accounts that did not have our equipment. The General Manager of The Commonwealth Serum Laboratory was my point of contact. I had secured an appointment straight off the bat with him and was feeling pretty happy with myself.

On my initial visit I shared with him my story about being new to sales, how I had been given all the non-Xerox accounts and how I was excited about the challenge of working with his organisation and helping his business be more productive. His was a similar scenario to one of the larger government departments with which I had also been successful in helping only the week before. In his gruff and disgruntled manner, he launched straight into a tirade of abuse, complaining about the level of service he had received, or not received, from Xerox over the years. He asked why I would be any different. I had a choice. I could have listened to him and his story and continued on with what I had been taught in sales training, or I could have listened to him and really heard him. I chose to put the sales process on hold.

We both spoke. He spoke, and I spoke, and then as I was half way through a sentence, he put his hand up and stopped me. There and then, he asked me to quote on one lone copier. Being so fresh and green, I didn't even go back to the office. I thought he meant he wanted it straight away. The innocence of the new kid on the block!

I sat in his foyer, hand wrote a proposal for one copier and walked back to his office, knocked on the door and asked to come in, proposal in hand. To say he was slightly surprised was a complete understatement, and I wasn't sure if I saw a small smile appear or not. However, not being able to complain about this unusual level of responsiveness, he waved me in, still with his initial gruffness.

My proposal began with what was most important to him. What I call the 'give a damn' factor, and in this case, it addressed his perception around past sales arrogance. It followed with the reasons why his business needed to review their approach to equipment purchases, the disadvantages of not changing and the advantages of shifting the status quo. It focussed on the impact this would all have on his business, and on him in his role as a General Manager.

Halfway through delivering what I thought was a real work of art, he stopped me again. He put his hand up and proceeded to tell me in no uncertain terms to *'go back to Xerox and tell Manager X and Manager Y that it was about **bloody** time they put someone on my account with a bit of enthusiasm who didn't just talk about themselves and how good they were.'* I turned that account around to 100% Xerox that day with a deal for thirty-five copiers.

The point to this story is:

- Was I the best seller in the world? **Absolutely not!**
- Did he remember the speed of the copier or how many sheets of paper it held in its document feeder, or why it was better than the competition? **Absolutely not!**
- Did he feel he was in safe hands, that he could trust me and that I was authentic in my approach! **Absolutely!**
- Did he believe, through the insights I shared from a previous rollout a month earlier and in his decision to back me, his organisation could improve productivity and profitability? **Absolutely!**
- Did I hear the problem behind the problem and the story within a story? **Absolutely!**

It was no different to selling stationery sets door to door – the story lay in the meaning behind the product, the emotional leverage gained through story and the relevance in its delivery.

There is power in being OK with who you are, not needing to be the owner of all things knowledgeable, to listen for what is being said and not said, and to frame their story in a significant manner.

So often sellers will make themselves the hero in the story.

Too often sellers will rely on their logical approach and not venture into story, transparency or vulnerability.

How to Bring Vulnerability into Business

Brene Brown shares, *'Vulnerability is the birthplace of innovation, creativity and change.'* When you can share experiences or mistakes that might have caused you, or others, to be less than perfect, it reduces fear and allows connection and change to happen faster. It helps remove the attachment around what other people will think.

I'm not suggesting you bare the skeletons in your closet, although that exercise with key people in your life outside of business might actually help you within the business. I'm talking about sharing parts of your experiences, and other client's experiences, within business conversations.

Let me give you an example that I have shared earlier in this book. As an owner of a small to mid-size business, we went bankrupt. Do you think being able to share that story with business owners, within a relevant context, might create a bond deeper than rapport building normally does? Do you think they might realise I know what challenges they face? Absolutely, it does! This story of mine does more for my buyer than any amount of problem defining, left brain questions and features of my product ever will. It creates enormous trust.

What is Your Value Story?

The major reason we want to use story according to the Clayman Institute, is because stories are remembered up to 22 times more than facts alone. If you can't manage to be agile enough today to switch brains when you need to from left brain to right brain and from statistics to story, then you won't truly uncover the real buying criteria. The real buying criteria is always emotional, and stories are the connective tissue within our emotional muscle.

We need to wrap story around an idea for that idea to stick and be compelling enough for people to act. Even in a courtroom, the best story will win the case, regardless of whether the defendant is innocent or guilty, as history has proven time and again.

Business or not, stories are about moving people.

When I was at Xerox we needed to know the speeds and feeds of not just every single one of our photocopiers, but our competitor's products too. I don't ever recall a customer asking me for any of those specific details, nor do I remember ever getting a deal based on those details, although I probably thought at the time, reeling off this information was the reason for winning the deal. How wrong was I?

According to the Sirius Decisions Sales and Marketing Summit it was revealed that approximately 71% of sales leaders believe that a seller is not able to articulate their value effectively. They also believe being able to do so separates high performers from low performers which means less than a third of commercial conversations have any value to the buyer at all. That's a problem.

Your value story is, therefore, another form of story.

How do you articulate your value story if it is not to be about product? Your value story should focus on who you are serving and the difference you are helping achieve.

One of my clients in New Zealand sells directly to the medical profession. Their value story is that they have products that *provide more nursing time.*' It is simple, relatable and invokes curiosity. That value story, in turn, provides fast and rapid ordering systems and makes the clinic run a lot smoother and of course, the patients benefit. It is such a simple statement and paints a picture. It tells a story.

One of the most common questions I get asked to help sellers and business owners with is, *'What is my story? What do I say I do? How do I frame the fact that I am a salesperson? or how do I elicit information without people thinking I am there to sell? What is the story I tell at a networking event that makes me feel authentic but doesn't short change my value yet generates discussion and respect? What is the modern-day story that replaces the outdated elevator pitch when I meet a prospective buyer?'*

Rather than tell people the story of what you do without any form of reference or context, or rather than reference your vignettes from the Messaging Matrix straight off the bat, ask a couple of high-quality questions about them instead. Make it about them. Start with a question, not a statement about you, so you at least know to whom you are talking.

It's a simple formula. Follow the pattern below and simply change the content. Add in your buyer's role and their responsibility and then articulate their issues, not forgetting to share an outcome that is measurable.

YOU: *'Do you own a business, or lead a team, or have a responsibility for generating revenue?'* I might say this to a someone I'm meeting for the first time [and you will have your own buyer persona] If they say *'no'* then I know they are not my target market.

Of course, if they do fit that persona, they will say *'yes'* to the question. From a psychological perspective, you have also placed them into what is called a *'yes'* framework which is a natural step in the rapport building process. You've made the conversation about them, you have engaged them, and they'll more than likely be more open to continuing the conversation.

The next part of the conversation is where you would introduce their main motivation. Areas that you know are challenges for them, or trigger points, and you would phrase this as a question, as well. This ensures that they say *'yes'* again. For example, let's assume I am talking to the owner of a business, or a sales leader responsible for generating revenue, I might now say,

YOU: *'Have you ever experienced or been concerned about your salespeople **not making budget** or **not being able to differentiate themselves** from the competition?'*

Within two questions you have now painted a picture and allowed them to tell their story. Your next flow in the conversation naturally shares what you do in context to those two answers you received.

YOU: *'That's exactly what I do. I help business owners in the manufacturing space who aren't making their numbers and don't know why and who want to differentiate themselves, yet don't know how. My clients all experience amazing top line growth.'* It's combining two stories into one and is very natural, human and powerful. And you will notice these answers are all vignettes and soundbites from your Messaging Matrix.

It's not about selling your features, advantages and benefits as you have done in the past. It's not rabbiting on about you and feeling awkward. It's a simple formula that creates a pull momentum as opposed to an unwelcome push approach.

Identifying a buyer's emotional buying criteria is something you cannot get from a spreadsheet. You can only get that from a story.

The next chapter leads you into asking those high-quality questions once you're prepared to take your conversation to a deeper level. It creates tension, the right kind of tension, which strengthens your prospects ability to buy into the emotional criteria of their buying decision.

SELF REFLECTION

How challenging do you find **not talking** about your product or company is on a first call?

Easy	Need More Work	Challenging

What do you believe are the 3 major advantages of being able to tell compelling stories?

1.

2.

3.

Create three stories, case studies or metaphors you can put in your toolbox to demonstrate value to a buyer and position you as an expert in your field.

1.

2.

3.

In the early 19th century, they tried selling soap as healthy. No one bought it. They tried selling it as sexy, and everyone bought it.

Rose George

CONSULT

THE ART OF TENSION

It's more than asking questions. It's creating a space to get personal, to be bold, to push the boundaries for all the right reasons and to create change in our clients' worlds.

T HE MANAGING DIRECTOR of the retail fit out business looked at his screen to see what appointments and meetings the day held ahead for him. He noted with anticipation a meeting with an old colleague over breakfast, followed by an overdue phone call to a long-term client who was having a few difficulties with his deliveries. He then saw a name that was unfamiliar, checked in with his assistant to understand who he was meeting, and more importantly, ask why he was meeting? She calmly commented, *'It's Joe Masters from The Maximus Company and I think he wants to speak with you about new retail fit outs.'*

At that moment, a prickly feeling came over his body, and his shoulders dropped. *'A seller'!* he thought. *'I'm too busy today.'* True to his word though, he kept the appointment and mustered up the state change needed to greet this guy and give him the benefit of the doubt. *'Maybe he might be different, and I might learn something new',* he thought.

The seller walked into the brightly lit, partitioned office, complete with full floor to ceiling window with a stunning panoramic view of the city. Waiting patiently for his newly connected potential buyer to enter, he looked around at the simplicity of the office and thoughts of how he would open the conversation raced through his mind.

Seconds later, in walked a casually dressed guy, quite unlike the suited vision this seller had pictured, and in an equally casual way, greetings were exchanged in an air of light heartedness. As they sat down, the seller was then asked a direct question by the potential buyer, *'So Joe, what can I do for you?'*

The suddenness of *'getting to the point'* caught Joe off guard and he *'lost his place.'* As a result, he began to wing the whole sales conversation, launching into what he and his company did, and sold.

Who was feeling the most tension?

We know the seller was. He was probably feeling nervous, or uncertain, underneath that exterior bravado.

But there was also tension from the buyer. Something a seller never considers. The buyer probably didn't want to speak to the seller, just as many of our buyers don't want to speak to us. They have been conditioned by the stereotypical sellers of the past, knowing a barrage of tell and sell will undoubtedly occur.

And our seller in this scenario fell right into that same old trap. Buyers expect different today and when they find a seller who is not in the mold of the old, but can create some anticipation, they will welcome you with open arms.

Lowering the Bad Tension and Lifting the Good Tension

We have to be mindful that our buyer is on a journey just as much as we are. Our role is to lower our tension by connecting with ourselves more and shifting **our** state, and it is also to lower the buyer's tension. To shift **his** from a state of **apprehension** when he first meets us, where is defences are up, to a state of **affirmation**, where he is aware of why the conversation is occurring and is OK with it. We have his trust and it's like he's given us the key to tap into what's important. With quality questions, insightful discussion, **exploration** of both challenges and objectives, our ideal is to generate a state of **anticipation** where we've unlocked what's really important and can move the conversation to the next logical step. It's where we create leverage and buy-in as outlined in the following Qualification Quadrant.

THE QUALIFICATION QUADRANT

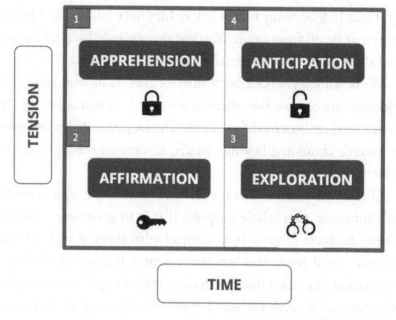

©Bernadette McClelland

Our ability to build rapport in those first few seconds and truly connect is crucial, because when we do, we actually lower the negative tension, especially from within the buyer. Unfortunately for many sellers, when it all looks favourable and there is strong rapport, they mistake this as a signal to jump straight into a product pitch or they lean on their technical knowledge without any form of exploration or qualification. The buyer puts the walls back up, trust is ruined and the ability to create the right kind of tension, anticipatory tension, disappears. You then become part of a commoditised conversation and it is then harder to get back on track.

This is where most objections begin - not at the end of the conversation. However, the buyer won't share those objections with you until you actually get to the end of the conversation. At the point when you ask them to make some type of decision.

Worse still, if the buyer doesn't give you an objection, he'll tell you instead that he'll get back to you before promptly disappearing into that black hole so many buyers before him have fallen into. Never to be seen or heard from again. Meanwhile, you're left scratching your head thinking, *'Why?'* Especially when *'we got on so well'*.

We've all experienced both sides of this coin. The reasons for objections are because the seller has not asked enough questions, Not created leverage, not qualified, definitely not uncovered or unlocked, the buyer's emotional buying criteria, or created the right kind of tension.

Our intention is to not only serve our buyer, it is also to disrupt their thinking. Our whole purpose, if it is to genuinely contribute to their business growth, is to connect with them at such a logical **and** emotional level, that we create a **new** tension. A tension of anticipation. A tension that has the buyer thinking, *'I want to continue this conversation with you and I won't mind paying.'* A tension we personally have experienced when we can't wait to open the door of our new home or turn the key and start the engine in our new car.

From Chit Chat to Business Speak

There comes a point after that initial connection, that small talk and rapport building, where the formal dialogue begins and the core of the conversation amps up. The biggest hurdle my clients face, as sellers, is making that transition from rapport building and small talk to business talk.

A simple approach is to be open and transparent and call it as it is: *'My purpose over the next thirty minutes is to understand more about your business and also to see if we are a fit in helping your sales team increase their revenue potential. I'd like to ask you a few questions first, are you OK with that?'*

Quite honestly, people who have the role of decision making like to get to the point fairly quickly, and they expect sellers to do the same. Namely, in two key ways:

1. By positioning themselves in a commercial manner
2. By asking intelligent questions and sharing commercial insights.

If a seller doesn't go into a sales conversation with a clear outcome for themselves, nor have a purpose for the buyer, guided by questions and statements to keep them on track, then they risk losing control of the conversation. In essence, it relies as much on preparation as it does on being agile, nimble and dancing within a sales framework. Quite simply, it's about reading the play and peppering the conversation with human-ness and deliberate intention.

Author, Og Mandino says, '*Take the attitude of a student, never be too big to ask questions, never know too much to learn something new.*'

Questions form the most important part of any seller's toolkit, because when you ask quality questions, that's when you'll hear the answers you want and need, in order for both parties to progress down a mutually beneficial path.

For the really astute, they can hear what is also **not** being said, by their preparedness to plan their questions and be totally present to the answer.

The Foundational Framework

There are many trains of thought when it comes to the consultative, questioning stage of the conversation, and there have been a plethora of studies and a mountain range of books written on the subject.

Whether your experience is TAS (Tactical Account Selling), PSS (Professional Selling Skills), QBS (Question Based Selling), SPIN (Situation, Problem, Implication, Needs Payoff), or the recent gamechanger, CHALLENGER, at their core are solid questions that extend past the product itself.

SPIN Selling, born in the 1980's after Neil Rackham researched 35,000 sales calls, elicited the strategies used by the most successful sellers. It became a staple framework for the sales profession identifying a rock-solid framework and expanding the seller's attention to detail and alignment to the buyer's needs.

Rackham realised that the most successful consulting skills included understanding the buyer's status quo, identifying explicit and implied needs through problem-based questions and then highlighting the impact these had on the business. It allowed the buyer to link the problem and solution to the deeper and broader business objectives.

All good stuff. Except the customer today is not only ahead of the game, he already knows his problems and his solution, and he expects us to know them as well. The last thing a buyer wants is a professional seller wasting their time by asking questions they can research the answers to themselves. The last words they want to hear are:

- 'What keeps you up at night?'
- 'If I had a magic wand, what would you do differently?'
- 'If I could... would you?'

What was extremely effective in the past is nowhere near enough today. Most sellers either aren't aware that a shift has happened, or they simply don't know how to make the shift themselves.

The days of 'Caveat Emptor' have now been replaced by Caveat Venditor' – from *Buyer Beware* to *Seller Beware*. If a seller does not know how to even begin to shift the thinking of the buyer, then how do they think they can disrupt the status quo of that buyer's business.

Disrupting the Buyer's Thinking

Sellers were, and still are, conditioned to find the pain of the buyer. Give them a headache and be the first one to hand them a Panadol. But today many buyers have self diagnosed their own ailments and are already researching and self-prescribing their own solutions, because of the benefits afforded by technology.

Once the buyer has created a short list of providers and vendors that they are satisfied with, (either suppliers who have demonstrated contribution and value though their branding, positioning and endorsements, or vendors whose voices have been shared through the reach of social media), then they will approach that supplier or vendor when they're ready, and not the other way around.

And when they make that approach, they expect the questions to be further along the process. They expect that conversation to be deeper and more stimulating than focussing on a few basic situation and stock standard, run of the mill discovery questions. Buyers of today want to have conversations around *'what if's?'* and *'did you know's?'* They want to hear competitive stories of ways they can go to market more effectively. They want insights into an outsider's view of their industry, and they want questions that make them think.

So, if the 21st century commercial world is shifting toward a more stimulating, intuitive, connected and authoritative based approach as we know it is, who does the buyer want to spend time with? What does that seller look like, sound like and act like?

This brief manifesto written on behalf of a buyer to a seller, provides an insight:

Sellers – *It doesn't worry me that your sales process is not perfect, so long as you help me think differently, help me be better at what I do. Do that, and you will be adding value to my role – anything else and you are like everyone else - boring, vanilla and beige.*

Sellers- *Be generous! Go where your competition fear to tread and give me the extras. The extras, the overs, the information, the ideas, the shortcuts, help me help **my** clients, because it won't be long, and your competition will be! We now expect the extras.*

Sellers- *Be a Leader! You don't have to be THE leader but show up with a guiding light for me, interest in what I do, a desire to help me help my buyers, bring to the table the same care factor for my challenges as you have for your own. Hone your personal leadership, thought leadership and sales leadership qualities, and lead me through the conversation. Know to let me lead you, too.*

Sellers – *Thank you for challenging my thinking and not backing down by being a 'yes' person. I need to know you won't change your stance when I cross question you. I need to know I can trust your character and your judgement, no matter what!*

Sellers – *I appreciate it when you can hear what I say simply by listening to what I don't say. Not many of you have that gift – the gift of sensory acuity. Just like not many of you have the gift of* *acknowledging a mistake or recognising and remedying it immediately. And while we are talking gifts, the gift of taking feedback is paramount.*

Sellers – *I am just like you. I don't like being 'sold to', I am wary of sellers overusing all those canned and predictable words with me, like productivity, reliability and versatility. I like to hear new words that are flavoured with growth and contribution, certainty and consideration, that are collaborative yet prescriptive.*

Sellers – *Learn the art of social online **and** offline. Embrace the art of storytelling that surpasses your features talk. Upgrade our conversations past consultative to contextual, and above all put meaning over the money and you won't need to default to discount.*

Sellers – *Know WHO you are before you walk through my door. I love working with someone who is comfortable with who they are, someone not intimidated by me, someone who is keen to share their art with the world because they are proud of their value and legacy. Someone who knows their WHY and what that means to me. Someone not desperate to be liked and expecting to be respected instead.*

Sellers – *We will follow you on your journey, we will treat you as trusted advisors when you converse with us, humanise a mechanical, predictable and industrial process called 'selling', speak **WITH** us, not broadcast **TO** us. We really do need you in our lives and we are willing to reciprocate by paying well those who serve us well.*

Sellers – *Have you seen this ode, internalised its words, absorbed its meaning? When you realise it's not about the sale, that it's about you and me, it's about give and take, breaking rules and building respect, that it's about commerce and business and economics based on the world we both live in. Then, if so, we are looking forward to working with you!*

How many of our clients speak to us about upgrading their aging equipment, adding another product line or replacing a broken widget? Their problem is never the equipment, product or widget even though that may be the presenting problem. Their problem is what that replacement **means to them.** They are buying themselves; they are buying the deeper problem your solution fixes. Your role in consulting is to find what that deeper problem is and create an air of tension that has them wanting to move toward a better scenario or move away from an existing one. It has an element of psychology, not text book selling.

As Albert Einstein quoted, *"No problem can be solved from the same level of consciousness that created it"*, and because our buyers have their own unique problems, more often than not they can't solve these problems themselves. The real value created, is to stimulate and help them think differently. To disrupt the status quo of their thinking, and to enable that is to own the quality of your questions.

Questions that Decode Our Buyers Thinking

Each of us, within our DNA at a very micro-level, run two strategies that motivate us. One is a *'moving away from pain,'* or *avoidance* strategy and the other, a *'moving toward pleasure,'* or *achievement* strategy.

Let me paint a picture. A great personality many of us are familiar with is Carl Lewis, nine times Olympic Gold medal winner. Let's understand why he wanted to win the gold medal. As shared in an interview, it wasn't to be the best, or win the medal or even relish the accolades an Olympic win might provide, as many of us might think. In his case, what motivated him was to **not lose** the medal, and therefore not disappoint his family. This is a great example of someone running a *'moving away from pain,'* or *avoidance* motivation strategy, as well as a great race!

And our buyers are no different. In listening to their thoughts, their reasons for doing things and their stories, we need to listen for whether our buyer is someone who wants to *'move away from'* problems and challenges, or if they are someone who wants to *'move toward'* solutions, possibilities or a better outcome.

You might think not every buyer has a problem to fix. That they buy because they want to, or maybe because they are an early adopter. However, there will be a driving motivation that is more than likely based on a subconscious strategy of *'moving away'* from a problem, that leads them to an achievement or outcome that they want. Let's consider the diehards that queue up overnight in all kinds of weather to buy the latest Apple product or those people who camp out overnight to get the first tickets to a concert. They don't appear to have any problem or challenge to overcome, they seem to simply want the first phone or front row seats. We would be forgiven for thinking they were motivated by *'moving toward'* or achieving an outcome. However, we could also be very wrong. What is motivating them is the actual reality of **not having** the latest phone or **not getting** the first tickets. This desire to **not miss out** is so strong it catapults them to doing whatever it takes to achieve their outcome or goal.

As salespeople, it is important our questions talk to **both** types of motivations.

The Carrot and the Stick

To give you another example of a *'toward'* and *'away'* strategy is the carrot and the stick scenario. The carrot is an example of a *'moving toward'* strategy. For example, *'If you make budget you will win the trip overseas.'* The stick is a *'moving away from'* strategy. For example, *'If you don't make budget we will halve your commission.'* Different approaches will drive some people to perform more than ever, and others, not at all.

We all have a natural tendency to lean one way or the other. In fact, the greater population is motivated by the fear of losing something. Instinctively, people will do whatever they need to do in order to move away from some kind of pain, or to avoid something that could be problematic, or something that causes fear or risk or uncertainty. Why? Because it's biological and neurological. Our ego steps up to protect us from harm and to keep us safe.

Whilst most of the world's general population operate from an *'away from'*, or *'avoidance'* mindset, the sales profession attracts individuals who are usually go-getters, visionaries and brave souls who want to talk about the latest and greatest. People who are motivated by the pleasure of *gaining* something tend to *'move toward'* and to *achieve* an outcome.

Both types of people are equally motivated in their own way. However, leverage is strongest when we have a challenge so painful that we would do anything to move away from, or avoid, it. Once we get enough leverage, then moving toward a goal, or a solution, or some kind of outcome we want to achieve, becomes easier.

It's almost like we have to go backwards to go forwards.

Being aware of our own natural tendencies is critical. I, for one, am a person who naturally moves towards possibilities. If I talk around the benefits and potential of what could be in the future, and my buyer is the opposite to me and is fearful about leaving the comfort of their status quo, then there will be a disconnect. If my buyer is concerned about what is **not** happening now and wants to fix a problem today, then we won't be on the same wavelength unless I adapt my thinking and behaviour and hang around in the avoidance and problems phase, or I validate his cautious thinking first before leading him toward a solution.

We all skew our questions toward our own natural motivational strategy, so adapting is crucial if we want connection to be stronger, and if we want to create leverage within our sales conversations. We have to embrace both styles, and like learning any new skill, this requires we work a different, cognitive muscle group.

Leveraging Strategies

Understanding the strategies you personally run will help you in addressing the needs and wants of your buyer. It will also make sense in you understanding what questions to ask and the reasoning behind those questions.

One of my clients asked me how I determine which strategy my buyer operates from when I first meet them. One of the first questions I ask in building rapport with a potential client is, '*What is it that caused you to meet with me today, apart from the fact I asked you*

☺?' Their answer will tell me. They will either be interested in how to improve their sales team's performance and sales results, or they'll be interested in ways they can rectify certain challenges or problems. One strategy is 'moving toward', and the other 'moving away'.

Knowing that is critical for me in knowing how to frame my questions.

It helps me discover what pain they may be in first, rather than discover what is working best for them or where they want to end up. It is easier to move to a solution off the back of an understood problem, because you will have more leverage by addressing their pain.

If you do what the majority of salespeople do first off, and share the advantages and positives, such as telling your buyer how good your product will be for them, you'll not create any emotional leverage and the conversation will remain on a logical level, no matter how helpful you think you are being. This is what makes your product irrelevant in the big scheme of things - because no emotional tension has been built. Therefore, no leverage is created.

It is critical that you understand both 'moving away from' and 'moving toward' strategies. Brainstorming a library of both types of questions will help your level of confidence and also help you concentrate more effectively in a client meeting.

Forget About Benefits for A While

The biggest shift of all is to undo a portion of what we have been taught for years and that is to rely on the benefits of our product. Unfortunately, when we do that then we are doing all the telling. It is also us assuming that what we think are the benefits are what the buyer believes to be the benefits. Could we ever be wrong? Absolutely!

The key is actually in our **questions** and our products **advantages**!

When we reverse engineer our questions using the advantages of our product, then the buyers relay back to us, in their own words, the **benefits** *they* will receive from our products. *Our* story becomes *their* story! The hero becomes *them*, not *us*! The telling is done by *them*, not *you*!

It's like we become conductors of the orchestra – or magicians!

To do this seamlessly, we need to get clear about a couple of meanings. Let me state the obvious for a moment.

- The feature of our product is what it is.
- The advantage of our product is what it does.
- The benefit of our product is what the buyer sees as the value to them.

So, why on earth would we put our own bias on sharing the benefits?

We must start with the advantages about what the features of our product do.

My suggestion to you right now is to create three columns. Column One is the feature of your product. Column Two is the advantage and Column Three is the benefit you offer. You will need to complete that exercise for each product and each feature to give you a breadth of questions.

It's about getting familiar with the **advantages** because you are going to need to reference them in your questions. You probably already are but in the wrong way. You are more than likely leading your conversations by **telling** the advantages. We need to stop doing that.

By creating a list of features and advantages we can ask the buyer what **they** perceive to be the benefit or advantage of being able to do, or have, whatever your product does, or has (which is very much moving toward a solution). We also need to ask them the downside or disadvantage of not doing, or having, whatever your product does or has (which is very much a moving away from solution). Once they answer, we can then take the questions deeper and broader to really understand their buying criteria and help them articulate it as well.

Here are some examples of both:

Away from Pain Questions:

'What would the **negative impact** be for you if you **weren't able** to….print your reports within a two-hour block?'

'What are the **frustrations** you feel when you are **not able to ….** market your brand online direct to your target market?'

'What **disadvantage** do you see when you **can't** …. understand what the gaps really are in your sales team at a mindset level?'

Toward Pleasure Questions

'How much **more effective will ….** the ability to break down grease in one hour instead of two hours be?'

'What are the **positives** surrounding a … having a cup of coffee that stays hot all day?'

'What **goodwill** is generated when …. you can offer a money back guarantee to your clients?'

In both styles and in all examples, whatever they answer, is through **their** filter, not yours.

The buyer then **tells you** the benefit surrounding your product, or they will **tell you** the disadvantage of not having what you provide.

One group of questions is moving away from loss, money, pain, inconvenience or time. It is moving away from the disadvantages of *not having* something.

The other is moving toward gain, convenience, more money and increase in energy. It is the advantage of *having* something. Once we understand this concept then we can dance within any sales framework.

Be mindful that the style opposite to your own style will be the hardest to grasp, and you will more than likely find yourself defaulting to your natural style more often than you want. It takes practice.

Stop Second Guessing

Creating a library of questions does two things. It ensures you connect with your buyer linguistically, but it also means you won't always be wondering what question to ask next. It means you can be totally present to any conversation, thereby elevating your listening skills and increasing your levels of conviction. It means you won't be driven by those fly-by-the-seat-of-your-pants emotions and you will be seen as the expert that you are.

It also means you will be able to hear what your potential buyers *aren't* saying. Having that ability to be flexible and agile, you will have more control over the conversation every time.

People buy on emotion and back it up with logic, which is why understanding what is really important to the buyer is critical. What you want to do is discover what is important to the buyer at that deeper, personal level.

What's Missing Though?

If you notice though there are two areas missing.

1. The lack of mention of your product and
2. A very important question that taps into the emotional part of the equation creating real leverage. That being knowing the type of buyer you are dealing with and the personal impact of the decision on him or her.

Firstly, too many sellers hear there is a problem and they think that's the green light to head straight to the solution. They think they can fix it straight away, and they dive straight down the rabbit hole and start talking product and solutions, because they think to themselves, '*YES! Here is an opportunity to sell*'! This is a trap that will either cost you the deal or lengthen the time it will take to win the business.

Secondly, if we realise we buy on emotion, then effectively we all buy who we are. We actually buy our identity. We buy what every outcome means to **us**. If this is the case, then it makes sense that the next step after we have understood the impact of the challenge on the business, or we have understood the upside of the offering to the business, is to discover our buyer's **personal** buying criteria.

Getting to The Emotional Buying Criteria

It's about asking our buyers what the **pain** of not having, not doing or not being something, means to them or the business? Alternately, it's about asking what the **gain** of having, doing or being something, means to them personally? And also, what will that continued pain or gain ultimately lead to in the future?

Let me give you a scenario:

Let's say Bob shares with us that if he doesn't market his brand directly on line to his target market, then it is going to negatively impact his lead generation.

When we then ask Bob what that negative impact on his lead generation means to him, he tells us his pipeline won't be enough to make target. When we ask him what that might lead to, he says reduced cashflow.

Who has done all the talking? What do we know about Bob? What does Bob know about us?

How about another one. Let's take Mary. If we ask Mary what being able to break down grease in one hour instead of two hours will do for her, she tells us she will get more floors cleaned in less time. When we ask her what cleaning more floors in less time means to her personally, she tells us she can leave work earlier. What does that lead to for Mary? Who would have guessed – picking her child up from day-care earlier.

Who has done all the talking? What do we know about Mary? What does Mary know about us?

Bobs' real concern is cash flow, and Mary's real concern is time spent with her child.

That's pretty transformational. That's more than doing a deal. That's making change happen. That's taking things from a hard sell from days of old to a heart sell in this new *Connection Economy*.

And we got there in three simple, yet very powerful, questions!

Once you understand your buyers emotional buying criteria, and the buyer realises you understand it and that you *'get him'*, he will trust you and be keen to hear whatever you have to say next. They will also pay a little more for what you offer, and price will virtually never be an objection.

We want the buyer to **deeply** understand the implication of the problem and create leverage by having the buyer feel a sense of urgency about changing the status quo and we want to create tension that is anticipatory and forward thinking.

Remember, the problem of the equipment, the product or the widget is not necessarily the real problem. There is always a story behind the story, and another problem behind the problem. It's your job to identify both.

This is what your buyers appreciate, *'I'm looking for an advisor. I'm really buying people not product. I want the sales person to advise me on the challenges I will face and how to overcome them. Those sales people earned the right to call at the executive level'* (BobBeck.com: 2006).

If we understand that we all make decisions on an emotional level and back it up with logic, then the business logic must be based on our T4 model - awareness around the **trends** of the industry, the **triggers** of the business and the **tasks** our buyer is responsible for. However, when we go deeper with our buyer and tap into the emotions – ultimately the decision making is based on an awareness of the **type** of person our buyer is and their identity.

- Did I make the right decision?
- If I have to present my spending at the Board Meeting in front of my colleagues, will it be acceptable?
- Have I met quota, so I look good for that promotion?
- Will I be safe in my job, so I can remain the family provider and protector?
- Does that mean I get to stop taking work home and can leave earlier to pick up my kids?
- Will I be able to retire?

By being aware of this scale and depth, you position yourself as an authority in your field as well as demonstrate you are someone who genuinely has your buyer's best interests at heart. This is how, as a seller, you make change happen on so many levels and impact lives, not just business outcomes.

Every issue will relate back to the human-ness of the conversation if we allow it.

Ask Additional Questions with E's

Finally, as part of our chapter on 'Consult – The Art of Tension, I've always said we should give SPIN selling a bit of a **spine** and ask even more questions with ease (E's).

Questions that are *envisaging* that take the buyer into the future. You might want to ask your buyer to imagine the scenario in three months, or six months or even in a year into the future, what the staff will be saying, or what he will be noticing once they have installed, implemented or rolled out your solution and what the impact will be? By doing so allows the buyer to connect with his imagination and see, hear or feel the outcome as if it had already happened. Once again, our imagination is so much stronger than our logic.

Questions that are **expansive** allow you to extend the conversation and let the buyer do all the heavy lifting while they do all the talking and you do all the listening. To do this you need to simply remember two tiny, but powerful, words that elicit so much more information: *'What else?' 'Who else,' 'How else?'* Practice those and you will soon realise you don't need to talk all the time.

Questions that are **emotive** are powerful, especially when there is that huge, invisible elephant in the room, when no one knows what to say. How many of us have sat in a meeting and realised that the opportunity was going south, and we haven't had the courage to call it for what it really was? A train wreck!

An emotive question is powerful, such as *James, I have to put my hand up here and take full responsibility. I am sensing we're not on the same page and if there is a problem, I'm wondering, would you give me some feedback. Are you OK with that?'*

Questions that are **elegant** and framed in such a way to diffuse any potential misalignment. Questions that begin with *'When...'* will frame a situation and put a conversation into context elegantly, without you having to be blunt. An example, *'When you mentioned earlier that I hadn't covered the main issues, is that something I can come back to you with, or have I misunderstood the request?'* So much more elegant than, *'Will you let me have another go?'*

Questions that are **economical** are a key part of any commercial conversation. If you can't ask these questions with ease, then you will be wasting your time and everybody else's, especially if you eventually find they can't or won't buy. Asking economic questions that include their budget, how they measure return on investment, timeframes, who else is responsible for the decision, or discovering the buyers KPI's are all critical commercial questions. If a seller doesn't ask, then it is blatantly obvious they have their own challenges around rules, values and beliefs that they need to address based on acceptance, money and authority.

Questions that are *engaging* are usually precise and simple and based on childlike curiosity. The longer the question, the more open to interpretation it is, as is asking two different questions in one question. Keeping it simple is key. Asking people's opinions are always engaging, such as, *'I'm curious as to your thoughts around how selling has changed in your industry over the past five years?'* will always engage anyone in a conversation, anywhere. And, of course, substitute the word **selling**, in this example, with whatever is relevant for you and your client.

Whichever style of selling suits you, what is important is to understand what makes a difference to your buyer and how your offering aligns to their values and motivations. At the end of the day articulating and having buy-in on the difference you will make to their business and their lives will always place you in the driver's seat.

It is a seller's role to reiterate the value of the conversation from both a logical and emotional standpoint, through any consultative process. How you do that is by understanding the power of context and articulating the anchoring essence of any conversation. Everything must have a meaning and we want to make sure we are on the same page as the buyer and vice versa. In the next chapter we show you the simplicity of doing that through *the art of meaning*.

SELF REFLECTION

Which specific potential buyer do you wish to understand at a deeper level?

_____

To plan a consulting session, include the following in your checklist:

Practice what to say
- Identify a trend in the industry
- Identify a trigger event you can link to your conversation
- Identify three challenges your buyer might face in his role

Practice what to ask
- Create three moving away from questions
- Create three moving toward questions
- Ask what is important to them personally

Tension; mental or emotional strain; intense, suppressed suspense, anxiety, or excitement

CONTEXT

THE ART OF MEANING

It's not about what you think it's about. Its essence is in interpretation, variation, listening for understanding and being prepared to get it wrong.

IF I WAS to ask you what the following pictures, icons or crosses stood for what might you say?

A *red cross* stands for health or emergency.

A *crucifix* represents religious beliefs.

A *skull and crossbones* epitomise death or danger.

A picture really does paint a thousand words and behind that timeless phrase is a classic case of **less is more**. Apart from the obvious simplicity, it demonstrates context and context is *the circumstances that form the setting for an event, statement, or idea, and in terms of which it can be fully understood*. It allows an idea or a message to be communicated without any communication at all, and in a purposeful manner. It's why asking someone **what something means** to them is powerful.

Fix the Broken Windows First

Malcolm Gladwell, in his book *'The Tipping Point'*, talks about *The Power of Context* and how the physical environment we create for ourselves has a dramatic impact on the way other people behave. He talks about creating a more orderly environment by looking after the little things. Fixing *'broken windows'* as an example, has a huge impact on the big things like fighting crime.

Some of the *'broken windows'* sellers can fix begin with the smaller details. How they think, how they ask questions, how they package their ideas and how they sell their thoughts – all sitting under the umbrella of commercial conversations. Once you have a conversation that allows both buyer and seller to be on the same page, to agree on concepts and move forward, the next stage ultimately leads to an outcome where both parties win. It's a broken window, that when fixed, has a dramatic impact on the bigger conversation.

The Structure of Communication

The more detail you go into with someone and the more specific you get, there is more of a tendency to break, or lose, rapport. The more detail you go into, you also leave yourself wide open for disagreement and criticism. It's up to us to recognise that our content, our stories, our details, our features, advantages and benefits may be extremely important as a foundation, but we also need to recognise that there are other more important ways of communicating our direction, without getting bogged down into the specific details.

It's a bit like asking someone how they are feeling, and depending on who you asked, you immediately realise it was a bad move. Where they proceed to tell you every little detail about what is wrong with them, and all you want is a quick, socially acceptable, answer. Or when you ask for an explanation to something and you get the '*he said*' and then '*she said*', and then '*he did*' and '*she did this back*', when all you wanted was the short '*hey, what was the conversation about?*' answer.

In many cases our buyers want to engage in a higher-level conversation with us that doesn't include detail and cross examination. They want to be able to chunk the conversation up to mean something to them.

Context is nothing more than a broad framework that allows others to plug in their own interpretation on what we are saying. It allows people to '*get*' what you are talking about without you actually talking about anything specific. A little bit like the symbols shown at the beginning of this chapter. The messages speak for themselves. They are contextual. We '*get it*', without any words needing to be spoken or explanations given.

How many buyers are turned off because the seller is too specific, bringing product into the conversation too soon before any context has been established?

'No', the buyer says, *'we're not in the market for that yet?'*, or they'll fob you off with some other kind of excuse. Either way, they definitely won't engage in a deeper conversation.

It's More Than Listening

One thing people suggest you do to understand the meaning behind any conversation, is to listen more. However, what does that really mean? Because sometimes when you do think you are listening, you still get it wrong. Why is that? It's because you haven't picked up the gist of the conversation or identified what the conversation is **really** all about. As a result, you start talking about stuff, or content, or detailed specifics and default to a topic that is comfortable for you, yet irrelevant to your buyer. It's because you haven't created any *context*.

The following example happened to me and might help put context into context for you. Even though I thought I was listening to my client, I missed the boat. I had gone down a rabbit hole without clearly establishing what she meant.

Lisa was one of my clients and was talking about:

- doing more market research,
- connecting to more key people and
- scoping her opportunities

In the spirit of helping and providing value, I began to share with her ideas around social media, content marketing and referral systems. I assumed what I was helping her to achieve was exactly what she wanted because we had previously talked about sales, marketing and client retention. What I failed to do though was to contextualise the conversation. I failed to ask her what **she** meant. When she said '*more market research, connecting to more key people and scoping her opportunities*', what I heard was different.

Clearly, I was looking through my own biased lens, basing the direction of the conversation on my own assumptions and experiences. As a result, I overlaid the conversation with my interpretation of what I thought she wanted. Whilst I thought I was doing the right thing I gave her a whole heap of ideas for business growth that ended up being totally irrelevant – and not because they weren't great ideas, they were my best! And it wasn't long before I felt the energy on the phone drop to an awkward silence.

First, I realised what I had done and acknowledged I had got it wrong (**it**, being the context), and secondly, I backtracked. I asked her what was really important from her perspective. By me asking her this question, she brought a different meaning to the conversation. Aha! Whilst I thought '*more market research, connecting to more key people and scoping her opportunities*' would give her immediate business growth, she was wanting bigger picture strategic ideas around industry and competition - two totally different lines of thought.

Here's a gold nugget for you! I took it one step further. I asked her 'out of those two focus points that you just mentioned - industry and competition, what is your top priority?' Competition was her answer. Now we could get deeper into the conversation and guess what eventually got put on the table as topics to discuss? Sales, marketing and client retention.

Context matters!

Gwyneth Paltrow demonstrated a great example, sadly at her expense, of how meanings can be misinterpreted when people don't understand things In context. When she decided to break up from Chris Martin, she referred to the split as *conscious uncoupling.* Everybody was up in arms about her comment, labelling her as someone who thought she was *'too good to say she was divorced'* and asking, *'who does she think she is?'*

What she meant, but didn't say, was that once you split from somebody it can actually be peaceful and amicable. You don't have to hate each other afterwards, especially when the outcome will impact your children. As she told Howard Stern on Sirius XM Radio, "*I made a mistake in that I didn't give it context. Like, I didn't say, 'this is... a philosophy.*" Her meaning was well intentioned, but she hadn't explained it fully and therefore it was taken out of context. We all do this. Either by not framing what we are saying in the correct way, or by not hearing what someone else is really saying.

So, we need to check in often that we have understood what the conversation is really all about. Then we need to check in that we are on the same page by repeating back or paraphrasing to gain clarity. And it's perfectly OK to do this.

When you realise this distinction, you find you do start listening more intently, because you are listening for something more than the spoken words - you are listening for what the words mean and what the conversation is really about. What are they really trying to say? You check in, clarify and calibrate and if you misinterpret it, then that is OK – you catch it early.

There is no right or wrong, just a misaligned interpretation, so you recalibrate and move on together. It is OK to come from that space of not being perfect, of not understanding and of being vulnerable. It's ego that stops a seller from recalibrating and being prepared to get it wrong.

Get Out of The Weeds

We know it is important for us to ask questions in a sales call, especially around both challenges and pain, as well as finding out about opportunities and possibilities. It's also important we get specific with the buyer because we need to help them create leverage and shift their status quo. A huge part of the responsibility around asking questions is to uncover the impact or effect or implication of any change. To do that means we need to drill down and be more specific, as well as chunk up and be bigger picture.

Many sellers take the buyer's early answers as a cue to jump straight into solving the problem, proposing their solution and trying to fix things. Just like I did with my client, we jump in with our ideas on what we think they meant.

We are 50% correct when we do this.

The correct 50% is based on **our** interpretation. We are coming from our view of the world. So that can't be wrong.

The 50% where we have got it wrong, though, is that we haven't understood what's really important or what the impact or effect or implication means to the buyer.

As Steven Covey stated in *'The Seven Habits of Highly Effective People'*, *'Seek first to understand, and then be understood.'*

We haven't sought to understand and yet we are trying to fix things.

And how we truly understand is by appreciating what something means to both parties. We do that by chunking the conversation up to a higher meaning, bringing it into the abstract or providing **context**.

Too many sellers chunk the conversation down, down into the detail and specifics and they get stuck in the weeds. The weeds have no interest for the buyer. The weeds are where the seller gets stuck in the content and detail of their product. The weeds are where your competitors go first. Don't go there!

How Do We Represent Context?

When we contextualise something, we start by framing it. For example, when you think about your company's growth, 'company growth' is the overarching umbrella (or the context). Many factors can fit under that umbrella. There can be staff, competition, metrics or activity (these factors are the content) and they all contribute to the company's growth. The context (or umbrella) doesn't necessarily need to change even though the content may change. Most people dive into the content and start talking about the details first without getting agreement on what the overarching context is really all about and there's no coming back when this happens.

As an example, *'Mr Customer, we'd like a meeting to talk about our latest services we provide for recruiting your new staff'* could lead the buyer to say, *'We don't need to recruit anyone'* because he probably doesn't. Instead, what would be a better conversation starter, would be, *'Mr Customer, we'd like to organise a meeting to discuss your business growth.'* That idea would be more attractive, and buyer focussed, don't you think?

If we agree that the example of *'engagement'* is important to a team, then we can provide any number of ways to improve engagement. If we don't quite hit the mark with one of the content ideas within that conversation, we can always redirect the conversation because the context (engagement) has stayed the same. Given we still have agreement on what the conversation is about (engagement), we simply suggest a different idea or different *content* piece. There can be no right or wrong once you have the context or framework agreed upon. It's also referred to as chunking up and down.

Chunking Up

The term *chunking up* is where we bring people's thinking to that of purpose. It is where we reach agreement and build solid rapport, or in extreme situations lead people into a total state of trance. When we ask people what something means, or for what purpose they are doing something, or we want to know what their intention is, it is referred to as chunking up. We want to do this with high level, strategic conversations with decision makers.

Chunking Down

The term *chunking down* is where we bring people's thinking down to that of detail and specifics. Commonly referred to as nit picking this is where we don't necessarily want to take our decision-making clients, but it is a place that our technical or operational clients enjoy. Too much detail opens you up for disagreement and this is the level where arguments and objections occur. It is also where rapport, or trance, is broken. It is where we drill down too much when asking for examples, or where we ask someone to get too specific, too soon or where we ask too many questions.

Ideally, through the use of our left and right brain, we want to be as flexible as we can and chunk our conversations up as well as down.

Go into the abstract as well as the detail, move from the content back up to the context. Whoever does this well, will lead any conversation.

It's Never About the I-Phone

When you don't agree on context, conflict occurs. Typically, in any argument or disagreement it tends to be around some petty little thing such as who did or didn't do something, the colour of a shirt you wore at a party twelve years ago, or the date of great Aunt Mary's wedding. Maybe I'm being a bit flippant, but I'm sure you understand my point — it's always about the detail, the content, the specifics. However, if you chunk the meaning up, eventually you will gain agreement at a higher level, and you will find it has nothing to do with the 'who said what, the shirt or the calendar'. Arguments and conflict lose their power when you gain agreement on what things really mean.

My daughter had agreed to give my son her iPhone once it came out of contract. For free! Closer to the time there was a discrepancy around an outstanding $50 out of contract fee. Who should pay?

My adult kids, whilst nine years apart hardly ever argue, and before we knew it we had an argument on our hands. Sitting down with them at the dinner table, I first asked my daughter what was going on. Being more reactive than my son and with a raised voice, she proceeded to loudly explain what was going on from her perspective. I asked her what it was really all about, she answered and so I decided to chunk it up again, and asked her, *what else does it mean?* She ended up saying she didn't feel respected by the way her brother spoke to her.

I did the same to my son. Being a little more reserved, I must admit, it was a bit like trying to get blood from a stone. Nonetheless, he proceeded to tell me what his thoughts were. Once again, I asked him what it was really all about, and when he was able to give me some semblance of an answer I asked him, *'what else?'* He said he found it difficult to speak with her sometimes.

We now had a different conversation on our hands – respect and communication. Needless to say, they hugged, made up and we continued a normal family dinner.

However, nowhere in that fifteen-minute conversation, was the $50 or the iPhone ever mentioned. Why not? Because the phone was never the issue.

It's up to us as sellers to find the real issue behind the issue, or the real story behind the story – to investigate what something is *really* all about.

It's Never About the Price

In a sales environment, instead of arguments, there will be objections.

Why do objections occur? They occur when a buyer will give us many different *'specific'* reasons why he won't do business with us - too expensive, too late, have the wrong colour, size or dimension. But are these the real reasons?

In most situations we know we never lose business based on price. There is always something more, another meaning, and it's up to us to identify these. Objections are usually smoke screens for a hidden problem. This is why when a buyer does give you price as an objection, you need to ask them to put price to the side and you must clarity on *'what else'* is important to them. *'Mr Customer, I understand price is important to you, but if we can put price to the side for a minute, are you OK with me asking you a couple more questions to gain more of an understanding of what else is important?'* We need to introduce context and real meaning. It is hardly ever about price just like it was never about the iPhone.

A number of ways to gain clarity around context and chunk up can include the following frames:

> What I think it's really all about is.....
> To clarify what you said is....
> Given that you said xyz, it seems......
> In essence, this seems to be about.....
> So, what you are saying is based around...

Framing includes a certain amount of vulnerability. A transparency that allows you to check in and bring your conversation back to a level of agreement that not only buys you time to think, but also allows you to pivot. It allows you to move from big picture to detail and everywhere in between.

The Hierarchy of Ideas

The person who can travel between abstract and specifics, or big picture and detail as demonstrated in this model from the works of NLP (Neuro Linguistic Programming) is the person who will ultimately lead any conversation.

In Trance

Intuitor

Big Picture

Abstract—Milton Model

The Structure of Overwhelm: Too Big Chunks

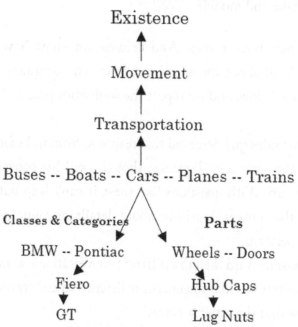

Existence

↑

Movement

↑

Transportation

↑

Buses -- Boats -- Cars -- Planes -- Trains

Classes & Categories   **Parts**

BMW -- Pontiac   Wheels -- Doors

Fiero   Hub Caps

GT   Lug Nuts

The Structure of Nit-Picking: Chunking Down and Mismatching

Specific — Meta Model

To demonstrate this model in real life, let's use an example of a car sales scenario to demonstrate the importance of context.

Let's go car shopping for a minute because we've all done that before. Let's walk onto a showroom floor and imagine the sales person approaches us and asks us some typical questions. What might some of those questions be? We've all been there so we know the questions tend to include:

- What are you looking for?
- What colour?
- 2 doors or 4 doors?
- Price range?
- Trade in value?
- Make and model?

We know how it goes. And because we know how it goes – because it's all about the specifics of the car, our guard is up, our level of trust is low, and we repeat the well-worn phrase, '*we are just looking.*'

Has the sales guy deserved that response from us before we even walk in? Probably not. Typically, though, will his conversation be about the car? With questions like these it can't help but be about the car – the content. It will be about details surrounding the car's ability to perform.

Let's fast forward then to a different conversation – a conversation that makes you feel like you are being listened to and where you have a knowing that the seller '*gets you.*'

'Good morning sir, how can I help you?' *I'm looking for a new 4WD*

'OK, what is important to you about a 4WD over a sedan?' *It's got to fit three kids, be reliable and have off-road ability.*

Most sellers would walk them over to the car and begin to explain how the car and its features are designed specifically for off road and for three kids. Don't be most sellers! Take it up a notch and remember your weapon of influence is your depth of question and the context those questions will elicit. We need to chunk it up.

'What would you do differently if you had a 4WD, apart from playing Dad's Taxi?' *We'd head to the mountains on the weekends.*

'And what would heading off to the mountains mean to your kids and your wife?' *It would give us all an opportunity to hang out together and see more of each other.*

'And what about for you personally – what would it ultimately lead to for you?' *It would get me out of the rat race and give me some much-needed time out.*

He's just told you what is really important to him. He has given you his emotional buying criteria – the context within which he will buy his next car. What's important to this guy is not how big the engine is or how economical the fuel supply is. If the car is aligned to his values, then he will justify it with all the logic that the size and economy offers him. We need to find out what his values are and to do that is to ask what is important to him personally.

I know whenever I have bought a car, it has always been a prestige car. Why? Because it makes me feel significant. As for the finer details, as long as it gets me from A to B, I'm OK with that. My husband on the other hand is driven by safety and that his family will be in no danger. Will our criteria be different? Of course, it will. Your role is to identify that criteria and you won't get it by giving someone a brochure.

The guy I have used in this example was in the hot seat in one of my workshops. He really was stressed and really did want to get away. *Time Out* was his real driver. We all buy ourselves first, before we buy anything else. A good seller knows that the decision to buy means something. He knows to stay away from the specifics in the beginning. He knows that *'content might be king'* but *'context – she rules the kingdom.'*

The Power of a Word

If we keep chunking up, apart from getting slightly annoying, then *getting away from the rat race and time-out* would eventually take this guy to *freedom*, which would ultimately, if we kept going, take us to *love*. The highest context we can get to is love, because ultimately everything is about love. I'm not suggesting you attempt to get to that level in your questioning – far from it! However, as sellers the more context we can provide, the more the buyer buys into his own interpretation.

From a linguistic perspective, words such as love and freedom and time out, growth and innovation, productivity and flexibility, are called *nominalisations*. A nominalisation is a word that is neither a verb nor a noun. I mean, what is **a freedom**? Or can you pass **the reliability** please. And words like reliability, freedom and connection aren't really what you would call doing words either, are they?

Nominalisations are words that are so abstract that people will put their own meanings on those words. Let's think about politicians. All they do at election time is talk smoke and mirrors or abstract vagueness, linguistically referred to as nominalisations. And that's why people vote for the person they vote for. It's because the constituents put their own meaning on the words that politicians use.

President Obama's 2004 presidential speech (The Speech That Made Him President) was, and is, a classic example of context. It was 100% a story of hope - something the country desperately needed and wanted.

Learn this Important Question

So, with that in mind, let's revisit our car salesman example. First though, let me ask you an important question. If love is ultimately the highest intention and purpose of us all, what do you believe the opposite of love to be? Most people believe it is the word *'hate.'* And they would be incorrect. The opposite of love is actually fear. Fear is the opposite of love, whilst gratitude is the antidote to fear.

Let's put that into context. Selling is one of the most highly mistrusted roles in the world, especially car sales, insurance sales and finance-based roles with *'85 percent of customers having a negative view of all salespeople'* according to the Brooks Group. This is because buyers have an immediate fear they will be conned, stitched up or manipulated. The main reason is because sellers love to tell you about their solution first without giving you a reason why or putting any context around it. They get too specific and therefore default to talking about the details of the product too soon. When they do this, it causes a psychological tension in the buyer, translating to fear.

What we are interested in is *'us.'* As the old saying goes, the most important topic on the planet is *'you.'* Your identity is what you buy. What are the conversations you are having with your buyers? Are they specific, feature based and stuff related conversations, or are they meaningful, abstract and contextual conversations that allow you to truly connect at an emotional level? What are those conversations really all about? What are you really hearing?

There are a few ways to have more value driven commercial conversations and here are some ideas you can play with:

- Listen for one second longer and let the person finish their sentence. Not simply for the purpose of hearing them out, but for the purpose of hearing what it really is they are talking about. It's only when we are not listening for the higher message, that we jump in, boots and all. Or worse still, start to plan what we are going to say next. Not only are we not present, we lose the thread and have no idea what the conversation is really all about for **them.**

- If we are able to check in and clarify what the conversation is **really** all about, and we get their agreement that we are on the same page, then we are in a much stronger position to lead them or give advice or suggest something that will help them. Checking in with our clients by clarifying, such as *'What I'm hearing you say is.....'*, or *'I want to check in that I've understood you correctly.......'* And if you find you've misunderstood something then congratulations! Because it will give you clarity faster. If you're told, *'No, what I mean is....'* that is the best thing to bring you back on track and then you will both be off and running again in the same direction.

- Have some key questions prepared prior, not just for the sake of asking questions, but to allow you to delve deeper, make you feel comfortable around asking personal and emotionally driven questions. Having well thought out questions will allow the other person to talk and share information you need to hear. It means they do the heavy lifting for you.

- Get comfortable with pauses, because inevitably that provides the other person with the space to process their thinking. You might even find you don't need to ask as many questions. Make the silent moments your friend and know that your question has caused your buyer to process and think at a deeper level. This is a good thing and will always take more time. We want them to take their time.

- And of course, you want to make sure you contextualise the conversation by confirming what you believe the point or idea is really all about. *'So, what this is really all about is [business growth, innovation, productivity].'* This helps you frame or reframe the conversation – it's a way to make sure you are both on the same page and therefore in agreement. Business is a process of agreement.

Models, Memory and Metaphors

Understanding *the art of meaning* is one thing. Capturing that meaning and articulating your commercial message is another. There is nothing more satisfying than sitting opposite a buyer and being able to understand and articulate their message and your own, in a manner that makes simple sense. It is a huge component of business acumen.

The art of commercial conversations is just a phrase until someone comes along and gives it a meaning, just as a jigsaw puzzle piece means nothing until the jigsaw is complete. The words around your product are just words until someone comes along and gives them meaning, too.

How we give something meaning and communicate that meaning, is to activate both sides of our brain. To activate our left brain, (logical and linear) and our right brain (creative and emotional).

Stories, metaphors and analogies, engage the right, creative side of the brain and will trigger communication, as we have shared in *the art of storytelling*. Metaphors are generally used when we say, *something is like something*. A bit like joining the dots or putting a square peg in a round hole.... Metaphors are the language of inspired, driven people and they allow us to create meaning by painting a picture in our mind. Of course, that last sentence was a metaphor in itself.

Steve Jobs once said, *'You can't connect the dots looking forward; you can only connect them looking backwards. So, you have to trust that the dots will somehow connect in your future.'* What is Jobs really saying? What is the meaning you are putting on that comment because chances are you will have made it mean something meaningful to you.

Models, on the other hand, activate the linear, logical and left-brain perspective and capture ideas just like the symbols did for us the beginning of the chapter. Generally, the language of process driven people, models could be represented with spreadsheets, boxes, quadrants, circles, Venn diagrams or time lines, providing context and meaning in a different way.

The ability to present an idea using both styles is needed today. There is nothing more powerful than a seller tapping in and bringing out the thought leader inside of them by capturing different ideas, making the complex simple and using either, or both, of these parts of their brain to help the buyer create greater meaning.

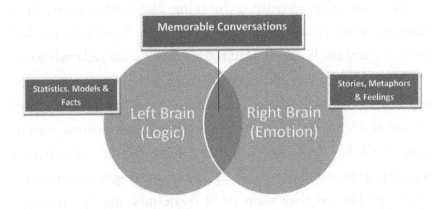

When the left brain uses models, statistics and facts and the right brain uses metaphors, stories and feelings, your commercial conversations make more sense and become even more memorable. Having memorable conversations differentiates you and separates you from your competition. They help you join the dots.

PERSONAL REFLECTION

- Are there moments when you feel you lose control, get off track or are not being as relevant as you would want?
  ☐ yes (if so, when?)
  ☐ no

- Create a list of frames you might use to bring the conversation up to a meaningful level, so you get even more buy in from the buyer.

Sometimes your greatest strength can emerge as a weakness if the context changes.

Harsha Bhogle

BOOK THREE

SELL!

THE VALUE TO YOUR MARKET
AND YOUR
SALES LEADERSHIP

CONTRACT

THE ART OF THE ASK

*It's not about closing the deal. It's about learning the language of **yes** and learning the language of **no** and understanding the magic that happens in between.*

I ONCE REMEMBER someone say, *"Bernadette, the answer is always no, unless you ask"* and I have always remembered it. If I am lost in the car and can't get the directions right, I will stop and ask someone for help, whereas my husband would rather keep driving until he finds the right road - and dare I say, wastes time and gets frustrated in the process. If I am seated at a restaurant that is near the door and it's a wet and windy night, I will ask if I can move, whereas a friend won't want to be an inconvenience and is miserable all night. If I feel that something is not quite right in a conversation, I will intuitively and subtly call the elephant in the room, whereas another seller may let a potential issue go through to the keeper, and in doing so attribute an incorrect meaning to the conversation. Most of us feel uncomfortable, not just when we challenge someone's thinking, but when we ask someone for help.

Amanda Palmer is a living statue whose job was to sell her art by standing on a milk crate, dressed as a bride, handing daisies to passers-by and connecting with them as they hopefully, tipped money into her hat.

All of us have seen these street artists, and some of us immediately jump to the conclusion that they may be beggars, or bludgers or even losers, as they stand in the popular tourist spots attracting passers-by.

But whose story is that - theirs or ours? And if it is our perception, then how does that belief serve us when it is **our** turn to stand on metaphorical milk crates and sell our products, services or ideas.

You see their story is that they allow people to **choose** to buy their art. If we, as sellers, are also artists then we want people to buy what we believe will make a difference in their worlds – in the form of our products, services or ideas, and we want them to choose us.

What does the street artist really sell? How does that compare with what **we** really sell? As I see it, they sell *connection* with the people whose eyes they look into as they stand statue like still. They sell *trust* as they reach out to complete strangers, and they also sell *vulnerability* by placing themselves in a position of potential rejection without having the luxury of slackening off for a few days to get over it.

Aren't we, therefore, the same as them? Are we not asking for our buyers to tip money into our hat? Are we also not asking our buyers to buy *our* connection, *our* trust and *our* vulnerability as we suggest they invest in increased profitability or improved productivity though us?

Amanda's story as a street artist complemented her life as a musician. When her recording company reported her music sales were diving, she took to social media and launched a Kickstarter campaign. Once again, she connected to the public. This time she opened herself up to the global market, trusting everyone with her crazy idea and was, yet again, completely vulnerable in asking for as much help as possible. With a target of one hundred thousand dollars, she proved that people really will help when they see a valid reason in doing so. Breaking a Kickstarter record, over 1.15 million dollars was raised in one month, clearly demonstrating *The Connection Economy* is alive and well – not just from a technological level, but a human level.

It proves that when we can exchange one form of value for another, people will oblige and reciprocate, but only if they see value. Asking for help is a vehicle; it is a currency for growth.

The *art of the ask* crosses all parts of our life - from within our relationships at home to how we run our businesses.

If we consider the simplicity behind the *art of the ask*, it's about:

- Getting intentional about your outcome and what you want to achieve
- Asking the right, purpose driven questions with clarity and precision
- Sharing the benefits and value on offer **to** others, and **for** others
- Helping people identify why your outcome is so important to them so they can emotionally create buy-in for themselves.

Robert Cialdini in his book '*Influence: The Psychology of Persuasion*', shares the principle of Reciprocity through an experiment undertaken with a university student. Instead of standing in a queue waiting to do his copying like everyone else, he had to ask the person at the front of the queue to let him in. The experiment criterion was based on two pieces of information:

1. He only had a couple of pages to copy and
2. He was in a rush.

Students were used in two different scenarios across two different universities to compare people's reactions when asking for help. More people gladly allowed those to jump the queue when they were given a reason, i.e. *'May I come to the front and use the copier for these two pages because I have a deadline to meet and will miss it if I don't'*, versus those who simply made the request by asking, *'May I get in front of you so I can use the copier'*, without giving a reason.

What this showed is that in the art of asking, when we give a reason and frame it well, when we put some context around it and people can see a reason *'why'* and align that *why* to what is important to them, it encourages the person we are asking to oblige. This is because, as part of human nature, we ultimately want to help others and contribute to their success.

Just as Amanda Palmer believed she was giving and receiving, her ability to be vulnerable and ask for what she wanted was made simple by that belief of reciprocity.

When our intention and mindset is based on an exchange of value, then commercial conversations become artful. It's no longer about making people buy, *'it's about **letting** people buy'* as Amanda so eloquently says.

Shifting Goal Posts

So where does it all fall down? Why is it that sellers get themselves tied up in knots when it's time to ask for the business? Why do they feel they have to whisper the words, get tongue tied, or worse, discount as a way to justify asking the question?

In days gone past, it used to be that the **ultimate** outcome of a sales call was to have a signed order. However, whilst that is still expected business practice, it is most often the beginning of a new relationship and partnership outcome that is the new ultimate outcome. The goal posts have shifted.

What used to be the ultimate outcome in the transactional sales environment **for us** is now about contributing to the growth of our customer's business **for them.**

Unfortunately, in some organisations, so much pressure has been placed on sellers to *'get out there and do the deal'* or to *'get the numbers,'* that it can backfire. Business can actually be lost as a result of financially motivating factors and the one-sidedness of the seller.

It can also backfire on the morale of the sales team. No seller wants to be a rooster today and feather duster tomorrow. That *'stick driven'* motivation, that *'Always be Closing'* mentality, causes desperation and a complete values mismatch that serves no one. If a real leader can help their people focus on the real meaning behind asking the question, then long term sustainable success will occur for all parties.

When a seller has challenges around asking purpose driven and outcome-based sales questions, it shows itself in many ways:

- Some sellers cut and run because their beliefs drive them, and they just crumble at the eleventh hour.

- Some have taken on the belief that their role is perceived more as con artists than real artists and therefore feel guilty asking for a commitment or standing firm on their price.
- Some lose because they haven't been able to ask strong enough questions earlier in the conversation and get stuck with objections at the end, not knowing how to react.
- Some get stuck because of their limiting beliefs around money and therefore don't want to see the buyer, in their eyes, at a financial disadvantage.
- Some sellers don't stop talking and are really uncomfortable with silence.
- Some sellers don't want to be seen as sellers!

Don't Sweat the Small Stuff

So, what is it that makes sellers sweat harder than a gypsy with a mortgage when asking for the business? Is it the stereotypical image of Gordon Gekko with his slicked back hair and greasy hand shake ready to 'do a deal'? Perhaps it is the image of a confident and professional Gerry Maguire who has such a strong belief around money that he can articulate the value, negotiate fairly, hold his price, show you the money, with the conviction to say 'no' if he feels like it.

Then again, is it the deep-seated perception that asking for the order is like begging? That standing like a statue dressed as a bride in a public place, arms outreached, begging bowl in hand is shameful and vulnerable. Could it be that our perception of ourselves is what we believe to be our buyer's perception of us? That we, as sellers, like Amanda Palmer don't have what we classify as a worthwhile job either?

You can have all the tools in the world and all the sales training on the planet, but if you can't trust yourself and your buyers, or you don't believe they see value in what your message is, if you haven't made that first sale to yourself, if you can't ask for the order without feeling this similar discomfort, then you'll never succeed in sales.

Sellers tend to focus too much on **their** perception of the customers beliefs, and as a result too much emphasis is placed on *'what if the customer says **no**?'* In many cases, that's because:

1. They don't know what to say if that happens
2. They never believed the buyer would buy anyway

No wonder business opportunities are left on the table. Because what you focus on is usually what you get.

The Go for No Theory

'No' is something sellers ought to aim for instead of fearing it. What do I mean by aiming for a *'no?'* The sales environment is very familiar with playing the numbers game where the amount of calls you make and the amount of *'no's'* you get means you are getting closer to a *'yes.'*

What if it meant that unless you get a *'no'*, you haven't done the right thing by the customer? What if not getting to a *'no'* means you made the conversation all about you? Let me explain.

My husband sold cars year ago – back when the Caprice was a top line Holden model. Only thing was, he never, ever sold one. Not One! Why? Because he couldn't imagine anyone spending *that much money* on a car! And he was actually an advocate for the Holden brand. The result was he never even gave the buyer the opportunity to say 'no' to that particular model. He safely led the buyers to the next model down. To the model **he** believed they could afford because that was what **he** could afford.

And he is not alone. I have done the same thing at Xerox. I perceived my buyer couldn't afford what I couldn't afford, and therefore never presented that additional, upscaled option.

But imagine if you let the buyer decide whether it was a 'yes' or a 'no' based on **their** terms! How many 'yeses' do you think my husband and I might have got if we had given the buyer the choice? And how many 'nos" might we **not** have got? It doesn't matter. If we aimed for the 'no's', then the 'yeses' would have taken care of themselves.

I'm sure the owner of our local white goods store wishes his seller realised that before serving me recently. With money burning a hole in my pocket and the opportunity to upgrade my blender to be one with all the gadgets, the seller showed me three blenders and then said, *'This one is not as expensive, but if you want the expensive one I can discount it.'* And he hadn't even asked us **one** question!

WOW! Margins are declining, and it is supposed to be the economy's fault. Really?

Reassess Beliefs

Sellers don't need to learn how to *close a deal* or *negotiate a contract*, they simply need to reassess their beliefs around what value means to them and to their buyer. And don't get me wrong - it's not just salespeople, its business leaders and business owners, too.

Let's consider an example closer to home. Ajax Engineers Fasteners, the sole provider of nuts and bolts and other fasteners to the Australian car industry didn't need to discount. They owned the market! So why did they end up going into liquidation in 2006? Quite simply they created a race to the bottom by continually discounting *against themselves*. When overseas prices increased for all of their products, they tried to offset the 75% price increase for steel and ended up having no margin left to play with. It was too little, too late. They had lost their own race. And unfortunately, they are no Robinson Crusoe!

So, why don't we take the pressure off ourselves and better practice *the art of commercial conversations*? To be strong enough to demonstrate to our buyers that this is supposed to be a win/win/ win. A win for the people, the profits of both companies and the greater good as opposed to a win/loss where it's all about the seller winning and overcharging the buyer, or even a loss/win where the seller walks around on eggshells fearful of being screwed down on price by the buyer.

Imagine if our conviction and belief was so strong that we were prepared to walk away if the deal wasn't a fit. If we said *'no'* to potential buyers who wanted us to drop our prices and impact our margin? It's more than OK for us to drive business based on a platform of ethical values, and this approach is becoming more popular and common. Businesses are starting to be OK with walking away rather than have an unprofitable customer because the cost is not just margin. The cost is energy, time, reputation, productivity and stress.

We just need to take a look at the recent Banking Royal Commission in Australia where the cost of bad practices, greed, incompetence and lack of personal responsibility has been at an enormous cost to people, profits and the greater good.

The Importance of a Money Mindset

We've already addressed the fact that nobody grew up wanting to be a seller. Just as nobody grew up knowing how to understand what makes people tick. What seller says, *'put more prospects in front of me so I can be told 'no' more often?'* Nobody I know!

Imagine if you could comfortably articulate the value part of the conversation, as well as the money part of the conversation? What difference would that make? Imagine if more people had a predisposition and intent to really shift people from where they are to where they want to be, **and** they cared? Where they actually owned the real value of selling change - making a difference!

These changemakers are the archetype our buyers actually want to see as their vendors and suppliers today. They want to hear the words, *"How Can I Help You' build your business?'* And, if they are the ones who drive you down in a race to the bottom, then you have to ask, *'Are they worth it?'*

Proposing a solution, offering a price and holding that price by being able to confidently justify the value exchange is not so easy for some sellers. They lose the sale at this stage for three reasons.

1. Their mindset i.e. they have belief issues around money and value
2. Their skillset i.e. they don't know how to effectively ask the questions
3. Their mindshare i.e. they don't have any value as perceived by the buyer

In reviewing the thinking of the vast majority of sellers when it comes to negotiating, closing and asking intentional questions, it's interesting to understand the deeper beliefs present that many have been conditioned to believe since childhood:

- Don't ask people how much they get paid – that's personal
- Don't talk to strangers about money – that's none of your business
- Don't fritter your money away on non-essentials
- NO - Do you think I'm made of money?
- Penny wise – pound foolish
- Save your money for a rainy day
- You can't take it with you
- Easy come, easy go
- Money doesn't grow on trees

If you are familiar with any of these, then subconsciously they may be sabotaging your success. If so, the antidote is to replace them with more empowering beliefs.

Society tends to split into two camps - those that have and those that don't have. Which camp did you fit in growing up, or into which camp did your parents condition you to believe you fitted?

Chances are, like many people, you may have grown up with money being not as readily available as you might have wanted. Perhaps your Dad worked more than one job, or your Mum went to work, and you were a latch-key child. Perhaps you didn't get the latest toys, designer clothes or exotic overseas trips.

Turn Financial Beliefs on Their Head

I'm not suggesting because of that you have money beliefs that hinder your ability to get ahead in sales. In fact, many people who did grow up in environments where there was a lack of resourceful money beliefs, have turned those beliefs around and are now extremely financially successful.

The founder of Starbucks, Howard Schulz is quoted as saying, *"Growing up I always felt like I was living on the other side of the tracks. I knew the people on the other side had more resources, more money, and happier families. And for some reason, I don't know why or how, I wanted to climb over that fence and achieve something beyond what people were saying was possible. I may have a suit and tie on now, but I know where I'm from and I know what it's like."*

But for the majority of sellers, this is one of the beliefs holding them back from asking the qualifying and quantifying questions around budget, availability of money in the organisation, allocated funding, ROI and TCO discussions, finding new money and asking for the contract to be signed.

What can you do to shift that? Apart from gain more clarity around your own beliefs, values and rules, you can begin to realise that money is good. It makes the world go around. When you make incorrect assumptions and decisions on behalf of other people's spending habits, and you potentially stop a deal from being finalised as a result, it does not make the world go around. In fact, it slows the economy and doesn't help anyone.

To put things into perspective for you around the meaning of money, here is a short story:

> *It is a slow day in a little Greek village. The rain is beating down and the streets are deserted. Times are tough, everybody is in debt, and everybody lives on credit. On this particular day a rich German tourist is driving*

through the village, stops at the local hotel and lays a $100 note on the desk, telling the hotel owner he wants to inspect the rooms upstairs in order to pick one to spend the night.

The owner gives him some keys and, as soon as the visitor has walked upstairs, the hotelier grabs the $100 note and runs next door to pay his debt to the butcher. The butcher takes the $100 note and runs down the street to repay his debt to the pig farmer. The pig farmer takes the $100 note and heads off to pay his bill at the supplier of feed and fuel. The guy at the Farmers' Co-op takes the $100 note and runs to pay his drinks bill at the tavern. The publican slips the money along to the local prostitute drinking at the bar, who has also been facing hard times and has had to offer him 'services' on credit. The hooker then rushes to the hotel and pays off her room bill to the hotel owner with the $100 note. The hotel proprietor then places the $100 note back on the counter, so the rich traveller will not suspect anything. At that moment the traveller comes down the stairs, picks up the $100 note, states that the rooms are not satisfactory, pockets the money, and leaves town.

No one produced anything. No one earned anything. However, the whole village is now out of debt and looking to the future with a lot more optimism. And that, Ladies and Gentlemen, is how money and selling works.

The Meaning We Place on Money

On a more serious note though, if we hark back to some of the excuses that sellers make, many of them relate to money:

- The competition discounted lower than us
- Our prices are too high
- The customer has no money in the budget
- Our resources have been cut
- Our product is just a commodity
- The economy is forcing people not to spend and so many more.

If the seller was to put their hand on their heart and these excuses were brought into the light of day, they would see that it was their beliefs around value, and the meaning of the dollar, that was sabotaging their success.

For example, does the seller believe that $1,000 is a lot of money or not? If they think it is a lot of money, then how can they sell the value of a $100,000 solution in a confident and aligned manner, if this is their charter?

Get used to money. Get used to talking about money. Get used to increasing your value. Get used to lifting your price. Get used to asking them about their revenues, their profits, their budgets, their anticipated ROI. Get used to adding a zero to what you currently think is a lot of money. Get used to asking them, *'How Can I Help You?'*

We live in an economy that is changing at a rapid rate of knots. It's an economy that is removing the dogmas and rules of yesteryear with a new generation that have a fearless approach to asking for what they want. Where salespeople need to get their act together and get over rejection in a much shorter period of time to positively impact their competitive edge. Where women are becoming more prevalent by standing in their power and asking for their rightful place at the table. Where business today relies on connecting and asking for the business in exchange for products, services and ideas that are valuable and valued on many levels. It's an environment where the *art of the ask* is a recognised exchange of value.

When we come together with our buyers and are there to truly serve them, we create a new partnership, a new entity, a new movement of change. How you keep that momentum going, and growing, is to deepen and broaden the conversation to a different level. Join us as we spell this out on the next few pages....

Self Reflection

What are **your** beliefs around money?

1.

2.

3.

What might you need to shift to sell at a higher dollar rate?

Do you find it easy to say NO to buyers when they want you to discount?

☐ Yes
☐ No

Task: Choose a product you sell where you have flexibility. What is the price you currently feel comfortable selling at and increase that in 10% options until you twitch. This is your new price. Push your beliefs and hold your margin and naturalise *the art of the ask.*

We thought we had the answers, it was the questions we had wrong'

Bono

CONVERSE

THE ART OF CONSPIRACY

It's not about keeping in touch, customer service or moments of truth. It's about working together, joint ventures and collaboration.

A CONSPIRACY IS described as the act of plotting or conspiring, usually for an evil cause, yet the first known use of the word *'conspire'* was back in the 14th century. It derives from the Anglo-French *'conspirer'*, from Latin *conspirare* to be in harmony and *spirare* to breathe.

Business today, whilst undergoing a transformation away from the evils of greed and selfishness that history has especially shown us in recent times, has its achievement steeped in conspiring for the success of all.

The Connection Economy that we find ourselves part of today is all about acting in harmony toward a common end with a much-needed focus on growth and contribution. The only way we can do that is to connect to each other through quality conversations and that means really listening. Listening with an intent to understand, to be curious, not to be understood. It's about communicating and holding your tongue on the roof of your mouth so the person you are listening to says all they need to say, and until you have something worthwhile to say.

It's realising that we can process listening to 500 words per minute and we speak at half of that, so it is a natural default that we fill that gap with thoughts and ideas and things we must say, or do, that we don't really, truly listen. We don't process what someone else is saying and allow their words and stories to fill the gaps.

Malcolm Forbes, of Forbes magazine fame said it best, 'The art of conversation lies in listening." And I concur, because 'The art of commercial conversation lies in listening **and** hearing'.

Today, it's about taking our conversations to a deeper level and not just listening but hearing what is really being said, and what is not. It's not about more information, it's not about more knowledge, more data, more product specs. It's about deeper, purposeful conversations that conspire for the success of all – what I call Connectorship.

Connectorship is not just embracing our heads and our hands – what we think and what we do. It's bringing the humanity side of the equation into our work environment by embracing our heart as well as trusting those hunches – fully owning what we love and what we feel.

Business today is about bringing our whole self to the table. To be OK with who we are and who we show up as, to trust where we are on our journey and realise that there is something greater at play – the success of all.

Only then will our people, our purpose, our profits and our patrons align to our business community, our culture, our commerce and our colleagues, thereby leading a true business steeped in connection.

To do this, a business must be **collegial** where the relationship between people is built on an individual respect for each other. When coming from a strong emotional and heart-based intention and trusting intuition, a strong atmosphere of teamwork and co-operation can be created. It is where being OK with what you feel matters and be OK with trusting what you know. It's where your identity matters. It's an environment and culture where you can grow, be challenged, be listened to and accepted. It is an environment that allows you to show up as who you need to be in a manner that creates happiness and loyalty for those internal customers and spreading outwards to those external customers.

THE BUSINESS OF CONNECTION

© BERNADETTE MCCLELLAND

It must be **cultural**, where the real outcome of the business is purpose **and** profits, generating both meaning and money for both stakeholders **and** shareholders. It's an environment championed by leaders who are able to marry the emotional needs of their people with the logical thinking necessary to adapt and change. Strategy and tactics also come into play here for the success of both the business and the people. When having awareness around your people's personal goals and values ensures there is loyalty and alignment to the values of the organisation. This, in turn, creates real purpose for the individual and the business.

It must be **commercial** where the responsibility is to generate revenue, increase profits, save money, invest wisely and reduce costs. Where the tasks, tactics and strategies include finding, converting and retaining business opportunities. This happens at a developmental, financial and operational level where the key driver is a win for the company and the client. In an era of increased competition, it is important to have a clear path of 'this is what we must do' to survive and thrive, so that the business continues to grow and benefits all, through an alignment of those values.

It must be led by the needs of the **community** which, when prioritised, is the strongest factor to the overall success of any business – serving and contributing for the common good. It's about serving the internal clients as well as the external clients. The social responsibilities of the business to the community will continue to create ripple effects that ultimately impact the world. It's about accountability to objectives, creating more opportunities to ask, *How Can I Help You?*'

This feedback loop ensures loyal employees, strong leaders, financially successful businesses and delighted clients, so the cycle continues and strengthens, and success is sustained.

The New World

If conspiring for both our growth and success and our customer's growth and success is to breathe harmony into that relationship, then it presupposes that at some stage our starting point must have lacked harmony and our outcome, growth and success.

The very transactional Sales 1.0 era with its loud, manipulative and often times dodgy, *do a deal* approaches clearly did lack harmony and the right kind of growth. Whilst there was solid growth around commissions and top dollar, everyone was happy – except the customer.

The new way forward shares with us an economy that shifts from a world that is transactional and desperate, to one that is transformational and difference making. A shift from pure capitalism to conscious capitalism. To an economy that takes us from that *get a deal* mentality, to one of *be the real deal*.

This shift means that businesses, leaders and sellers are evolving from a hard-sell based approach to a heart-sell commercial conversation, and from a thought process of *what's mine is mine* to a *what's mine can also be yours, through an exchange of value*.

The 'Me to We' Environment

The rules of business are being rewritten.

When individuals, businesses or organisations conspire for the success of others a sense of partnership and sharing of ideas occurs.

Walls are broken down and trust and empathy prevails. As Neil Gaiman, Smoke and Mirrors writes, *"The irritating question they ask us—us being writers—is: 'Where do you get your ideas?' And the answer is: Confluence. Things come together. The right ingredients and suddenly: Abracadabra"*

Like the stakeholders in our personal and professional lives, we must become the changemakers that help bring together ideas to create change in our buyer's lives, that create change in business as well as the greater community, so that they, too, can say *Abracadabra!*

There is always enough for everyone in this world when we think past ourselves and think past what we want. Where we can collaborate based on what's good for all parties.

'Two sisters each wanted the same orange. They each thought they deserved the whole orange, yet they compromised and cut the orange in half. Collaborating in this manner allowed one sister to take only the peel and use it for her baking and so she threw away the pulp. The other sister ate the tasty pulp and threw away the skin.'

When we really get clear on what our buyer wants, we can collaborate based on real wants and needs and everyone has an opportunity to receive their fair piece of the pie, or the orange, even when there are two competing entities.

Going Against the Grain

If we don't value ourselves first, we won't be valued by others. If we can't articulate our value to others, they won't see our value, and if we don't position ourselves as valuable, we won't be considered invaluable in the market. The bonus is that when we get this right it equates to more recommendations, referrals and repeat business.

Years ago, in the 1980's, a colleague of mine, whilst we both worked at Xerox, was working closely with a customer while selling a high-volume photocopier. This guy was a successful seller and was well on his way to securing a sale with a large Sydney based university. He had researched his customer's environment, understood the business applications and was ready to present his solution. As part of his research, he uncovered a need the customer had that was crucial to the customer's business success.

The customer needed to be able to print onto A2 sized paper and the solution that Xerox had at the time didn't offer that feature on the particular copier/printer and he wasn't able to provide a solution. His alternative was to offer a lesser overall solution that did include that feature, win the business, get paid a healthy commission, or be honest with the customer and walk away.

Being a man of integrity, he chose the latter option. Not only did he admit the weakness in his solution and gracefully walk away, he went the extra mile. He provided the customer with the contact name of our competitor - the opposition company he knew could provide that solution.

The reputation that he built both personally and professionally was worth its weight in gold. This story has obviously stuck in my memory and even though my integrity has never needed to be demonstrated in such extreme measures, I believe in a values-based, conscious selling approach.

When you go against the grain, decline a buyer or explain to them you can't help, your attachment is not based on *what is in it for you*. When you refer them to another company, your competitor for example, who has options that you can't offer, your attachment is to *what's in it for the buyer*. This would usually be considered heresy by most organisations; however, the decision to align your values to business outcomes and intentions is critical.

Today this same guy has strong relationships with people in the industry and has positioned himself through trust and integrity, no matter what company he works with. His personal and professional brand and reputation has been, and remains, built on a solid foundation of conspiring for the success of others.

What Your Rituals Don't Do

As we are entering *The Connection Economy*, are we really connecting? Are we present in conversations? Are we truly listening? Are we relevant? Is our personal and professional brand congruent with what we are saying and doing? Are we actually moving people? If we're not moving people, we need to rethink our intention.

When we wake up in the morning, we have our own individual rituals that operate almost on automatic pilot. We then go to work, and in many cases, this same ritualised process flows into our business day. We do the same old thing, see the same people, speak the same things and think the same thoughts.

And then we come home, and the rituals continue. We greet our family with the same phrases, eat at the same time and relax doing the same things. Nothing changes.

Imagine, though, if we spent a couple of minutes analysing what we do and focussed on changing just one tiny thing to elevate our value to others. Because it's the little things that make the biggest difference.

Water gets hot at 211 degrees, it boils and creates steam at 212 degrees and steam can power a locomotive. What are the little things you can do to make a difference?

o Maybe you asked your customer an extra question such as *'How Can I Help You?'* in a particular area?

o Or maybe you asked them, 'What has been the value you have received from us lately?' to help them reflect on the value they have actually received from you.

o Or maybe you took time out to know, 'What matters to them most' in their role.

If we give time to our customer, then conspiring for their success is not difficult. For years these instances have been referred to as moments of truth.

Moments of Truth

Moments of truth is a term coined years ago by Jan Carlzon the CEO of Scandinavian Airlines System. He realised the power that the first fifteen seconds a passenger and a staff member had together could make or break them, and that still holds true today. What are the small differences you can make in the life of your client? What is the difference you are selling? Client relationships are what keep a business alive and in this *Connection Economy* we cannot underestimate *the art of conspiracy* for our internal customers, external customers and ourselves.

It's About Building Trust

When we consider today's buyer and what they want from a seller, they want someone who can truly sit on the same side of the table with them and work toward a common goal, both before the paperwork is signed, and afterwards.

The manipulator may enjoy the short-term success, but long-term buyers want sellers who care and have their best interests at heart. They want someone who can hold themselves accountable and are responsive and reliable in a trustworthy fashion.

So, how do you work together to have a greater impact on your buyer's world? The following are three megatrends occurring in business today when it comes to the *me to we* economy:

Co-operation is a process where people help each other. Co-operation can be seen in the simplest of things. One of my clients knows their sellers do a brilliant job of understanding the needs of the buyer, can gain commitment and is able to differentiate themselves by going above and beyond, but the silos internally are not aligned with the customer's real needs. As a result, the level of co-operation is limited, negatively impacts others and therefore, their results. We can so often point the finger and blame others for lack of results but if we make an individual shift, as well as a collective shift, in the simplest of ways such as thanking, recognising and validating those around us, losing the need to be right and getting caught up in politics, or simply listening to other's ideas, then the results could be very different.

Collaboration is a process where two or more people or organizations work together, and it results in mutual benefits for a shared goal, where everyone wins. If one company needs to grow revenue by selling a widget and another company is looking to partner with a company that sells widgets, then through a series of trigger events, two parties will conspire for each other's success. Due to the benefits of technology it may even mean you don't need to create an actual product anymore; instead you can share resources and once again, change the traditional rules of business.

The amount of business initiatives around customers and partners working together, has doubled over the past two years. Collaboration is one of the top five actions being taken by the surveyed respondents of a study done by the Aberdeen Group, and is becoming a high priority for businesses in combating rising costs.

Dr. Jaclyn Kostner in her book 'Knights of the Tele-Round Table' commented, *"Global companies that collaborate better, perform better. Those that collaborate less, do not perform as well. It's just that simple."* If we bring it to an individual level, those individuals that collaborate in groups that include families, business and social gatherings have more success, and less chance of being ignored those who don't collaborate at all.

Charles Darwin knew this years ago when he said, *"In the long history of humankind (and animal kind, too) those who learned to collaborate and improvise most effectively have prevailed."*

Since 2008, more than four million people have rented their accommodation from private individuals who have shared their personal resources - beds in spare rooms! A great example of collaboration in this new *Connection Economy* where sharing of resources and dollars is the key, has been successfully demonstrated by AirBNB, a San Francisco based company who, back in 2008, decided it was a great business idea to provides the database and backend resources to these home owners and it owns no real estate.

Uber, who has just posted a 2015 valuation of 50Bn, was a 2011 start-up and owns no taxis! E-Bay owns no stores! Everyone wins! This is collaboration at its best.

Co-opetition—a process of collaboration between business competitors in the hope of mutually beneficial results allowing businesses to expand their offerings into new markets or to simply survive an economical downturn. General Motors and Toyota both collaborated to design the same car and take them to market under individual names - the Chevrolet Prizm and the Toyota Corolla. Within the tourism industry, vineyards that are separate entities unto themselves, each vie for the tourist's dollar, yet bring their uniqueness to a collective table and promote the region as one. Within that collective, they each compete against one another, yet still collaborate.

I am a co-founder of the Sales Mastermind Australasia and Women Sales Pros, where a core group of competitors in the sales leadership space conspire for the success of the greater sales industry by collaborating harmoniously. It's finding a new way to do things. It's an example of innovation and marketing, two things every business needs according to legendary management consultant, Peter Drucker.

What Do You Bring to The Table?

It is all about what people can bring to the table for each other.

o   If you are active and relevant to your buyers, will they appreciate your efforts?
o   If you provide someone with a trial of a product and they like what they see, will they buy?

o   If you provide articles of value on your social media channels will they see you in a collaborative light?

o   If you connect one client up with another where they might be of value to each other will they include you in future discussions?

o   If you support a competitor on social will they reciprocate?

The law of reciprocity, the law of give and take, says 'yes.'

The *me to we* economy will contribute to growth, retention and levels of loyalty. It's about conversations based on an **'and, and'** mindset and not an, **'either-or'** mindset. It shows up when businesses give customers access to what happens behind closed doors, or when they drop their proprietary software and provide an open architecture, or when they create a customised solution based on specific needs or vary their financial arrangement, so the solution can be a drip-fed approach rather than expecting an all-inclusive upfront capex arrangement.

There are so many ways to collaborate with a customer. First, you need to understand their real needs and get clear about your own intention.

Intention is so important. What is your intention when signing a contract? Go back a couple of earlier steps, what is your intention when you first contact a buyer?

Sure, we all do a happy dance and high five the nearest person when we get the nod for a deal, but after that, what is your modus operandi? Do you palm the relationship off to someone else in your organisation, do you congratulate your new client in some way, do you sign the order and then front up three years later to resign the next deal, or do you plan a process that ensures they experience ongoing *customer delight?* Do you provide a plan moving forward that makes them feel good, so they don't experience buyer's remorse, so that things come together and *abracadabra* – you create an experience? Do you go deeper and broader with your conversations?

The Multiplier Effect

The multiplier effect is a phenomenon whereby a given change in a particular input causes a larger change in any output.

It is not rocket science. In the famous words of Zig Ziglar *'you can have everything in life you want, if you will just help enough other people get what they want.'*

That being said, *Customer Service* will get you in the door and *Customer Experience* will keep you there. When your intention is to do both, your reputation will precede you. You will be viewed as an expert in your industry through *your customer's eyes*, not yours, which is far more impactful.

When our relationships are strong and based on solid respect and accountability, it can't help but create ongoing business. The *lifetime value of a customer* equation comes into play with the multipliers being humanisation of an otherwise very operational and commercial process, collaboration through the sharing of ideas, insights and information and innovative ideas for the growth of all parties. The diminishers come into play when there is a misalignment of values and value. We all go to where we are valued, and our buyers are no different. It's our responsibility to make them feel valued.

Here are sixteen collaborative ways to ensure you operate from a multiplier effect. How many of the following are you practising in your business relationships?

- **Create a Vision** – Make sure everyone in the business knows what the end game is and that their intention to achieve that vision is aligned.
- **Know Who Your Buyer is** – The trends of the industry, the trigger events of the business, the tasks they are measured on, what they are responsible for achieving and the type of person they are.
- **Get Emotional** –Know their real buying criteria at an emotional level and not just the logical level, because less people will shop around if you understand their motivations.
- **Be on the ball** – if you receive a request or a call, follow up in a time frame that you have agreed is relevant.
- **Know your stuff** – Responsiveness is not just calling back straight away, it is calling back with an insight or next step forward.
- **Look the Part** – check that your appearance, collateral and outlook is aligned to the buyer's perception of value.
- **Have an Open Mind** – lose the attachment to getting an order and listen for what the customer is really saying – or not saying.
- **Build the Trust** – do what you say you will do, when you say you will do it and in the way that you know the customer expects you to do it.
- **Attention to Detail** – this is a great mantra shared with me over many years because the slightest omission can cause the biggest problems, complaints and loss of business. Cross your t's and dot your i's.

- **Beyond the Gap** – know what they expect in a relationship with a supplier, know what they don't want in a relationship with a supplier, and know that you can deliver beyond the gap.
- **Know the difference you are selling** – Are you aware of what your customers have really bought from you, outside of your idea, product or service – from their perspective?
- **Provide a Plan** – it is important to future pace the customer, so they know the care and attention they will get after the purchase, such as regular reviews, understanding your responsibilities and theirs, and ensuring communication is optimised.
- **Keep in Touch** – provide value on an ongoing basis and mix it up with a phone call, email, newsletter, social media posts, direct mail and referrals.
- **Create Advocates** – be so good that they need you in their business and they don't mind telling others they need you, too.
- **Be a Connector** – who do you know who could be connected to someone else to help their business?
- **Know Your Value** – The voice of the customer is critical so ask for more than feedback. Presuppose they are receiving value and ask them to share the value they are receiving.

The ultimate outcome as sellers and sales leaders is to contribute to the success and growth of the whole business, to have all parties breathing in harmony and to ensure it is not a zero-sum outcome.

If word of mouth, now world of mouth, was the vehicle that ensured your success, then how would your clients answer the following question of you, *'Would you recommend this company, person or product to a friend, business associate or relative?'*.

On that note, the next chapter, the last of the conversations and ironically called *the art of the start*, is the ultimate starting and end point for achieving our most human based outcome of all – contribution.

Self Reflection

1. Name your top 5 customers that you will ask, *'what value have I contributed to your business in the past month?'*

   1.

   2

   3

   4

   5

2. Create a Gant chart on how you plan to look after your clients in the next 12 months, who they are, what is of value to them professionally and personally, and what their expectations of a relationship with you are and aren't.

3. Write down one thing that you will do differently to conspire for the success of your clients even more?

   ....

   ....

   ....

   Once you make a decision, the universe conspires to make it happen.

   Ralph Waldo Emerson

CONTRIBUTE

THE ART OF THE START

It's not about the money or the profits or shareholders. It's about the meaning, the purpose and the stakeholders.

I N THE WORDS of T.S. Eliot, *'What we call the beginning is often the end. And to make an end is to make a beginning. The end is where we start from.'*

As members of the sales profession, our ultimate outcome is to make change happen. It is to sell change. Not just to move product and make our numbers, but something bigger. To move people – to make a difference!

Henry Ford said it the best, *"A business that makes nothing but money, is a poor business."* And we have seen the giants that have created the massive profits, purely for the sake of making profit, fall. We've seen their greed cause the financial world to collapse, and unfortunately a huge part of the collateral damage was every day families like yours and mine. They were everyday people just like you and me.

At the London launch of Richard Branson's book's '*Screw Business as Usual*,' he said, "*I truly believe that capitalism was created to help people live better lives, but sadly over the years it has lost its way a bit. The short-term focus on profit has driven most businesses to forget about the important long-term role they have in taking care of people and the planet.*"

Business today has a responsibility to do business responsibly. Business has a responsibility to be consciously capitalistic. And sellers have a responsibility to consciously sell.

'*Today, you are a rooster! Tomorrow you'll all be feather dusters unless you make your numbers!! So, stop your BS and get out there and bury the competition!*' Now, you'd be forgiven for thinking you were on the set of Glengarry Glen Ross decades ago, but these words unfortunately came from the boardroom of a fine Australian corporation, straight from the mouth of the General Manager himself in 2015. So old world! So, bullying and so completely self focussed! And while these leaders continue to sit at the head of business, the sales culture will never shift.

Contrast that approach with one of my clients, Northwest Pest Control Company in Atlanta, Georgia. They have positioned themselves as the leading company in their industry, and it is not hard to see why. Rather than keep all their success secrets to themselves, they invited the state's smaller pest control companies to share their success principles that have led to them becoming the experts in their field. Why? Because their bigger message is that they contribute to the greater good by creating healthier living and working environments for homes and businesses, and this sharing environment is an extension of their mission. They don't just sell pest and termite needs. Their outcome is to contribute. At every given moment these sellers are reminded of the values that are written on their foyer walls to the point they don't need reminding. They live them.

We all love a good news story and when a business disrupts the standard business processes and becomes human, we love the story even more. Posted on Facebook last week by a friend about to board a Delta flight from Atlanta to Washington, epitomising humanity in business, she wrote, *'Elderly gentleman at security this morning didn't know he couldn't take his favourite pocketknife on the plane with him. A Delta rep took the knife, pulled the man's checked bag and packed the knife for him. Nice service, #Delta'* It's about doing the right thing, not just doing things right.

Whose sellers will be more proud, passionate and paid up? Whose sellers will add more value to their current clients and have stories to tell their prospective clients? Whose sellers will sell more by moving people?

Business as usual won't cut it. Especially in the world of selling where the majority of leaders' mantras still include, *'Get the deal at any cost'*, *'Discount the deal before month end'*, *'Cut the margin and give them something to get them to sign NOW.'* And let's not forget those infamous steak knives either!

For business to step up a level there needs to be a shift in intention in both the leaders and the individual sellers for **everyone** to benefit on **all** levels. In the book, *'Conscious Capitalism – Liberating the Heroic Spirit of Business'*, the authors John Mackay and Raj Sisodia, espouse four tenets of conscious capitalism:

* Higher Purpose
* Conscious Leadership

- Stakeholder Integration
- Conscious Culture and Management

I think they are missing a standalone tenet,

- Conscious Selling

Ask yourself the following questions:

Are you just *doing a deal* and going through the motions dialling for dollars, instructing people on your product and then closing for the order?

Perhaps you are at a point where you have built caring relationships, where you influence people on what your offering can do for their business and spend a small amount of time just to keep the relationship alive?

Or maybe you are inspiring your customers, pre-empting their questions of *'what's next, what's new and what's different'* and going above and beyond to transform the partnership where you truly are serving them and helping with **their** profit building intentions?

What's it all about?

Selling today is not only about making money as it always has been. It is about making money with meaning, and that means getting clear on what is really important to the buyer, and the buyer's business at both a personal and professional level.

Businesses that are focused on more than just the money are the businesses that are creating immense loyalty with their stakeholders first, and shareholders second. They are the ones surviving through the tough times and holding their margin. They are the ones whose customers stick with them and who acknowledge the value they provide. These businesses are driven by their own personal values of what is important and not driven just by the sale. The rise of Conscious Capitalism, GameChanger 500 businesses and B-Corporations is testament to this values-based shift in commerce.

Conscious Capitalism has a foundation based on the premise that corporations, organisations and businesses work for the financial benefit **of** all of us, as well as the social benefit **to** all of us. The industrial revolution, whilst creating growth in the world, was also all about capitalism. Unfortunately, cheap labour abounded, lives were damaged, and the planet began to be polluted and suffer. To the minority, all that mattered were profits.

The economic environment of recent times has shown us how the financial greed of Wall Street lined the pockets of the modern-day powerbrokers. This negated the social responsibility of capitalism, creating a massive and disastrous ripple effect across the globe, epitomised in recent headlining blockbuster movies glamorising greed and narcissism, whilst providing us a quick and dirty sales lesson on how to sell pens.

Values Driven and Triple Bottom Line

So, what does this have to do with the new sales environment and changing sales landscape? After all, a company has a responsibility to make a profit through its sales force, doesn't it?

And yes, the answer is that capitalism does have its place. But it's about being more conscious, having a responsibility to make more than profits and to look at the triple bottom line of people, profits and the planet – add your patrons and purpose to that and it becomes a quintuple bottom line – aka Connectorship.

This is a shift many leaders are not sure about, on both a personal and professional level. And it's possible they are unsure, because to champion it, means standing for something. It means putting their head above the parapet. It means holding people accountable and aligning their professional values with their personal values.

And personal values for many sellers and leaders are unknown. Either they can't articulate their own values, they can't language what is important, or they won't allow personal and professional lines to be blurred. They can't be seen as too vulnerable, they can't let the mask slip, or they can't show their humanness.

Buyers today, though, want real. They want you to stand for something, have conviction and bring all of you to the table.

I mentioned my client Northwest Pest Control in Atlanta, Georgia earlier and how I presented to a room of their sales people. What really moved me was the way the morning started. The VP of Sales introduced the sales meeting in the usual business-like way and then asked one of the guys to lead the group with a prayer. Now when I say prayer, I don't mean *sit down, stand up, and pick a bale of cotton prayer* that many of us may have grown up with in a typical church environment. It was more a positive intention.

And as I am sitting at the back of the room waiting to be introduced, a question went through my mind, *'would this happen in any sales team in which I have been a member?'* and the answer was a resounding *'no.'* From a speaker's perception, I immediately felt I was in a really safe environment, free of judgment and total acceptance. I experienced no fear or apprehension and it made me wonder if that was how their customers felt.

Realness Rocks!

Imagine creating a culture where it was all about serving others. Imagine that there was a bigger intention, a purpose, the ability for a bunch of guys and girls to feel it's OK to be themselves, to be comfortable enough in their own skin, to be the same at work as they are at home, to enjoy and be responsible for generating revenue and at the same time have no attachment to it, feeling their personal values and professional values were in perfect alignment.

As an example, as recent as 5 minutes ago, a client asked me, *"Bernadette, when a prospect says they are really happy with who they are using, and I have tried a couple of different approaches and I can't win an appointment, what do I do?"* My answer was to respect their wishes and walk away. You aren't going to every have a 100% hit rate, just as you can't hold a gun to someone's head. I did add however, *"only after you have shared with him that because you respect his decision you'd like to keep the lines of communication open to keep him informed of what is happening in **his** industry from **your** perspective from time to time and ask him if he is OK with that."*

I suggest businesses realise the soft skills are no longer quite as soft as they once might have been painted out to be and are actually a foundation for the real hard results. It is only in recognising this and having the bravery to take the road less travelled in many instances that the leaders will be able to truly support and identify what is really preventing their people from achieving the results they are capable of achieving. By tapping into people's true abilities and strengths, toning down the alpha male traits, replacing language that epitomises hardball hunters and reducing competitiveness that dominates relationships, sales environments will become more humanised.

In the example I just cited, that particular buyer would **never** have bought from that seller had he kept hounding him. He might never buy from him ever, but he might one day be in a position to refer him, due to the value he added when he knew he wasn't going to *get a deal.* That is an example of genuinely contributing and conspiring for someone's success when there is nothing in it for you in the short term.

Long-term and sustainable relationships will develop when the stereotypical feminine traits of connection, empathy, intuition and care are nurtured. That doesn't mean we need to sit cross-legged in tie-dyed hippy pants singing kumbaya or rolling out our yoga mats. Far from it, but it does mean acknowledging and encouraging the potential of people.

British actor, playwright and novelist Chris Humphries said it best when he said,

"Nowadays true job satisfaction and happiness is about fulfilling your full potential, tapping into your own creativity and feeling that you can make a difference." We need leaders to make that happen.

The Value of Values

When your brain moves from a hard-core outcome focus to one of awareness and gratitude for your opportunities, when you envisage a difference you will make in your buyer's world, tomorrow, next month or next year, it kills all fear. Gratitude is the antidote to fear because the focus is no longer just about you – your focus is on others!

If businesses want their sellers to have **value driven** conversations with buyers, then they must start *at home* by having **'values' driven** conversations with their people. The business becomes the value creator. The business comes from a *'How Can I Help You?'* angle by providing a communal environment, creating a leadership culture and driving commercial activities with a focus on the clientele, both internal and external.

The sellers are the messengers. If you have a worthwhile message to deliver, along with the relevant support to deliver the message effectively, and within an environment of trust, they will deliver their best self, in that way, every day!

Do business leaders actually know what is important to the individuals that support their revenue generation?

Do business leaders really know what's important to their buyers, to their clients? Perhaps, this chapter might remind them.

Everyone Wins

When businesses operate with higher purpose over and above just the profits, they create value for all stakeholders. When real value is created and transferred, then discounting, tradeoffs, revolving doors and lack of loyalty are massively minimised, and in some cases completely eliminated. Clients know the real reason why they are needed, momentum is created, and everyone wins.

Lisa Earle in her book, *'Selling with Noble Purpose'* believes when a company has an NSP, or Noble Sales Purpose, that team will drive outstanding sales numbers. Her research is based on six years of interviewing and working with sellers who consistently outsold their quota driven peers, and it defined that they genuinely wanted to make a difference for their customers. As sales professionals they were totally authentic and proud of the difference they made.

In a recent interview article in Forbes, John Mackay, founder of Whole Foods and his research partner Raj Sisodia shared how companies who practice the tenets of Conscious Capitalism had investment returns of 1025% over the past ten years, even through the global financial crisis. This was compared to only 122% for the S&P 500 and 31% for the companies profiled in the bestselling book '*Good to Great*.' Combine that with a Nielsen survey where 43% of global consumers say they would be willing to spend more for a product or service that supports this cause, and we know it's time to rethink values, and consider cultural shifts.

Having a higher purpose, realising stakeholder integration, operating under conscious leadership, practicing conscious culture and management and having sellers adopt the conscious selling approach are not just tactics, buzz words, or strategies. It's not just an afterthought that displays and ticks the box for *Corporate Social Responsibility*.

Putting a real focus on having a purpose and living core values are central to the new contribution based, *Connection Economy*. It is being recognised in businesses that include TATA, Toyota, Southwest Airlines and Northwest Pest Control, as examples. Within Australia, a previously unknown company, once they started generating profits, began apportioning a percentage of each year's profits to charitable causes, primarily in Asia. That company is Intrepid Travel. Whole Kids founded by James and Monica Meldrum is another example of business owners driven by a dream to do business consciously by creating healthy snacks for the children they would one day have. Ten years and two children later, theirs has become a great success story.

BankMECU is yet another example of a 100% company owned bank where all profits go back into benefitting the customers. These businesses are creating environments where everyone wins – the people, the profits and the planet.

These businesses have sailed through the tough economic times that the world has recently gone through, running rings around other businesses because they created a database of advocates that stayed loyal. They have the mindset and intention to contribute to their customer's business growth, in addition to their own. They are transformational sales organisations.

Anyone can get out there and do a deal. Anyone can make money. It's when you can make money and create change in the world, in your community, in your customer's world, that's what will get your people out of bed in the morning. It's not about being the best in the world but being the best **for** the world. That's what will create a culture of contribution and have the market know the value you provide. That's how you build it and they will come!

Selling is a people game. And people will climb mountains, jump through hoops and give their all when they are doing something for a worthwhile purpose. The secret is to ensure you balance the growth of the people with the growth of the business.

The Real Meaning of SALES...

Little do people realise that the word SELL comes from the old English word 'sellan' which means 'to give.' And when you consider that serving someone is really what selling is all about, then it goes without saying that it be based on an intention to give. Just as we grew up with the mantra of 'charity begins at home', we want to create an environment where our customer feels at home with us. We can do that by asking, *'How can we help you?'*

To achieve an outcome that is based on the quintuple bottom line, where everyone wins, is a valid business objective. While the walls in foyers and boardrooms are adorned with framed mission statements and company values, many are never more than just that. Words captured, written down and ignored. They need to be executed as 'the way we do business today' with personal and organisational values aligned, and with buy-in from the top and the bottom.

In his book *'To Sell Is Human'*, Dan Pink tells us the story of the last Fuller Brush Man who believed in his heart, soul and mind that he sold more than brooms and brushes. He had an innate inner conviction that allowed him to believe he was *a crusader against unsanitary kitchens and inadequately clean homes*. He believed the sale of his product was not just providing revenue for his company; he lived the belief it had a deep and altruistic benefit for the buyer.

By definition, as sellers, when we get clear on what our strengths really are, when we understand the real difference we make and what our purpose is, we have the ability to make change happen on so many different levels.

We become true changemakers and that role is a privilege as well as a responsibility. Ultimately bringing us full circle to how we position ourselves exclusively, think laterally and sell consciously. True transformational selling and inspired leadership.

Reflection

What are your top three values as a seller?

....

....

....

To what extent are you a *giver* in your business dealings?

1...2....3....4....5....6....7....8....9....10

What are three ways you can help your client or potential client build their business more effectively and help them grow in their roles?

....

....

....

> *"Each of us is a unique strand in the intricate web of life and here to make a contribution."*
>
> Deepak Chopra

THE LAST SAY

The purpose of a business is to create a customer who creates customers.

~ *Shiv Singh*

S ELLING STATIONERY SETS for Multiple Sclerosis was my first sales role, albeit a part time and fun holiday job to fund my journey down the east coast of Australia when I was just eighteen years of age. But it was more than that. It helped children who couldn't do what I could do to live lives with more flexibility, purpose and hope.

Moving into the world of professional selling came a few years later. Whilst employed at Xerox as an order entry clerk, moving into the credit department where my role was to collect money from late paying customers, I made the move down the long-hallowed hallway to the sales domain, where my place on the sales floor was cemented as one of the sales secretaries. It was not much later that I was asked to be the sales co-ordinator and the opportunity opened up for the hiring of new sales trainees.

I raised my hand, not once but three times, and was knocked back each time, because *'I was too nice'* and *'I didn't have what it took to be in sales.'*

My third and final walk into the Managing Directors office showed that I did, in fact, have what it took. It demonstrated to me the importance of making that first sale to yourself and my career direction immediately changed. Goal accomplished! I walked out of that office and into my new role as sales trainee that very afternoon.

The biggest learning was that I was selling so much more than copiers. I was selling increased revenues for my clients by helping them increase their levels of enrolment by providing a higher quality output, I was helping them maximise their cost per square metre of floor space, so they could improve their work surroundings, I was helping them save time, so they could leave work earlier. I was never selling a copier because my buyer didn't want *just a copier.*

After reaching the role of senior sales executive for that same company, Xerox Australia, I changed direction again to pursue the role of mentor and inspirational speaker for businesses and people responsible for generating revenue. But you know enough about my thinking now, enough to know that I am not selling sales training. No, I am helping you shorten those sales cycles you have, helping you reach your targets, so you earn more money, helping you to get those products to market faster so you can get the edge and mostly make a difference in your life.

People in sales roles today, want three key resources:

1. They want help creating cut through in their approach
2. They want to know how to have *different* conversations that position them as experts

3. They want to be known for what they know and become experts in their industry so that their reputation precedes them

As professional B2B sales leaders there are three key things you can do immediately:

1. Own your own value. Make a conscious decision and decide to create some personal cut through and bridge that gap between actualisation and aspiration. Once you do, you will have a solid foundation to build upon. Remember though, the person who creates the problem can never be the one to solve it so find a coach, a mentor, a role model and work with someone - anyone!

2. Take time to understand your buyer's industry and their top three trends and challenges so you can lead and position yourself as an expert in any conversation. Not only will you demonstrate you speak their language, you showcase your expertise and interest, and by default, engage in a discussion that is of higher value than your product. They will respect you for that.

3. Learn to *go for no* more often, detach from the need to be liked all the time and lose the desperation of getting a deal. It's about respect not likeability. There is no such thing as perfection, yet so many people refuse to put themselves in positions of potential rejection, or worse, take too long to recover from that rejection. *Go for no* and you might just find more *yeses*.

And a bonus 4th idea - Gain clarity around what really truly differentiates you. It won't be your product – it will be your values, your message and the meaning behind your story. Tell your story!

I believe Steve Jobs got it right when it comes to encapsulating the meaning of selling today:

> "To me, marketing [selling] is about values,' he said. 'This is a very complicated world; a very noisy world and we're not going to get the chance to get people to remember us. No company is. So, we have to be very clear about what we want people to know about us."

Sales, per se, the economy and lack of opportunities are *never* the problem. The problem lies in the meaning you place on each of these. *The Art of Commercial Conversations* helps you place a new, more empowered and profitable meaning on what to do in order to drive revenue, increase margin and sell a difference in the lives of those you serve. More importantly, it all starts and ends with how you show up and who you need to be, sitting atop a foundation of five simple words, *'How Can I Help You?'*

For speaking engagements, SKOs, trainings and coaching of teams and executives please contact:

bernadette@bernadettemcclelland.com

or

open@3redfolders.com

or visit

www.bernadettemcclelland.com

or

www.3redfolders.com

Printed in January 2023
by Rotomail Italia S.p.A., Vignate (MI) - Italy